James *Barber's*
Immodest but Honest
Good Eating
Cookbook

Solstice Press
P. O. Box 9223, Moscow, Idaho 83843

To my mother, who deserves it.

Special acknowledgment and thanks to
Christina Burridge.

James Barber, 1971, 1978, 1981

Published by Solstice Press
Box 9223, Moscow, Idaho 83843

A Solstice Press book produced at North Country
Book Express, Inc., by Melissa Rockwood, Patty
McCauley, Karla Fromm, Mary Schierman and Jen-
nifer Brathovde under the direction of Patricia Hart
and Ivar Nelson.

Designed by Melissa Rockwood
Illustrated by James Barber

Cover design Melissa Rockwood

Manufactured in the United States of America

ISBN: 0-932722-12-1

10 9 8 7 6 5 4 3 2 1

Introduction

Most people don't cook because they're scared to. Plain and simple cooking has become a photographer's art. The easy and good stuff—the sort of stuff grandma used to make while holding a baby in one arm and a frypan in the other—has been crowded out by complicated gourmet food, made even worse by colour photographs of fancy food, accompanied by even fancier recipes, and served on plates borrowed from Nancy Reagan's White House collection.

Real people can't cook like that, any more than real people can look like the centerfolds in *Playboy*. And real food doesn't look like that—it has smells and textures and immediacy and hunger which can't be photographed. Time is an important ingredient in food: five minutes here, ten minutes there, while the ingredients marry themselves to one another, and the cooks relax. A photograph can't capture all that.

It ought to be cooks, not one singular cook, and it ought to be relaxing. Making dinner, like making love, is better when it's a shared activity, and best when it comes naturally. Good food, or food that's good to eat, is natural. The French fisherman's wife making a bouillabaisse doesn't spend two days shopping and another day dirtying every pot in the house—she cooks what's available locally, in her one and only pot, while her spouse tidies up the nets. They eat, and they go to bed. Voilà.

We have locally available stuff too. The supermarkets and the corner stores may not carry frogs' legs, size 8½ AAA, or imported nightingales' tongues, but they will have some fresh vegetables, some fruit, and some meat. Cooking those things is as quick and easy and a lot more enjoyable than defrosting a packaged meal in the microwave. Making dinner from simple ingredients, with simple techniques, is as relaxing, and a lot cheaper, than most traditional therapies.

And that fisherman's wife again. She's never seen a measuring cup in her life, and if her husband doesn't have a leftover lobster then she still makes her bouillabaisse—even if the only thing he has left over is an ancient codfish she still makes it. She improvises, and once again, like making love, it's never the same twice running.

This book is about improvisation. Ingredients—if there's no veal, use chicken. Quantities—measure by the pinch. Mistakes—make them. There are basically four recipes in the world—whatever you have you bake, boil, fry or screw up. The screw ups frequently taste best—things like the overcooked corned beef hash which develops that wonderful, crisp, slightly more than burned crust on the bottom; or the cinnamon you put in the stew instead of paprika, so that suddenly it's not a goulash but a Moroccan dish. Be arrogant about your mistakes to others, and honest with yourself. Trying to be perfect is the basis of being scared.

It's also about generosity. All those recipes that tell you to use 1/16 of a teaspoon of anything are suspect—they're not written by cooks but by cocaine dealers. Recipes in this book are all simple, most of them quick, all using easily found ingredients, all absolutely foolproof, and most important, all very good to eat.

Anybody who can cook things that people like to eat is a hell of a good cook, and doesn't need to be a *chef*—or have a matched set of silver-lined saucepans.

Contents

Breads, Desserts, Drinks

Clams Daniel

Daniel was a waiter. And Daniel liked to eat. He liked to eat a little more and a little better than most people. So he learned to cook. Which made him an even better waiter because when people asked him "What is.....?" he would tell them. They would be impressed because he had a French accent, surprised to get an answer, and generally grateful because waiters sometimes tend to put their noses on high beam and make you feel stupid.

Their gratitude made Daniel a lot of money: He decided to become a restaurateur, to open his own joint, to become the employer of waiters. And then make much more money, in much less time.

But Daniel found that it would have been easier to walk across Lake Ontario than to make money in a restaurant, and that operating a twenty-four hour day care centre would have given him more time.

Daniel now runs a fishing boat. He makes this dish for himself. He used to make it for his customers. Nobody knew it came out of a can.

And if you don't tell them either.....

Fry until transparent ½ chopped onion and 1 clove chopped garlic in 1 Tbsp olive oil. Add ½ tsp pepper and 1 can small clams (OR chopped clams). Heat quickly and stir a lot. Add juice of ¼ lemon, ½ tsp curry powder and 1 oz sherry. Heat quickly and flambé with scotch.

Hurry Up Clam Chowder

Fish Needs Fennel. Remember that. The most ancient, sad and dejected piece of fish in the world can be transformed by fennel into something exciting.

The little hard kernels need grinding up. If you haven't got a mortar, use two spoons. Put the fennel in one and the other on top and press hard with your thumb while you wriggle them about.

Dill is almost as good, but a better herb for shellfish. The fennel has a more exciting taste, which comes through the smoothness of the potatoes and clam juice.

This is not a prescription recipe. Onions are essential, and so is some sort of bacon, even if it is only bacon fat left over from the breakfast frying pan. Celery is nice, but so is green pepper, and so are thin sliced mushrooms, or even leeks. It is capable of almost infinite extension by the use of soup cubes. I usually feed two people with this amount. But if two or four more arrive there is always another potato, and another soup cube, and another cup of water. And another stick of celery and....

There is nothing quite like a wet afternoon dig-ging clams and coming home to a hot bath and clam chowder. Kids like it; fathers become enormously popular. After a movie or a walk it is a genuine half-hour recipe which is much more fun than waiting for the pizza delivery man to arrive with a bill for ten bucks and what you save on pizza you can spend on beer or a bottle of wine.

If you can't dig clams, then the canned minced ones are the cheapest and best alternative. Everything except the fennel is usually available in the corner store and if you want to plan ahead for a lot of people then get all the nice things you like for the chowder, and make garlic bread and put a dish of chopped parsley on the side and some one-inch lengths of green onion for people to dump in as they like.

Leeks in half-inch slices are very good in chowder if you want to make it a family meal. Fry them a little first in butter or oil or bacon fat. Don't worry about making too much—somehow it always disappears.

continued

Hurry Up Clam Chowder

Chop 3 slices bacon, 2 sticks celery and 1 medium onion into ½-inch bits. Fry bacon until transparent in its own fat, then fry onions and celery in the same pan until transparent. Add the juice of a can of clams, 1 bay leaf, ½ lemon, dash pepper, ½ tsp dill or fennel and ½ tsp curry powder. Add 1 chicken soup cube, 1 diced potato, 1 chopped garlic and 1 c water. Cover and simmer 30 mintues. Add clams and simmer for another 5 minutes.

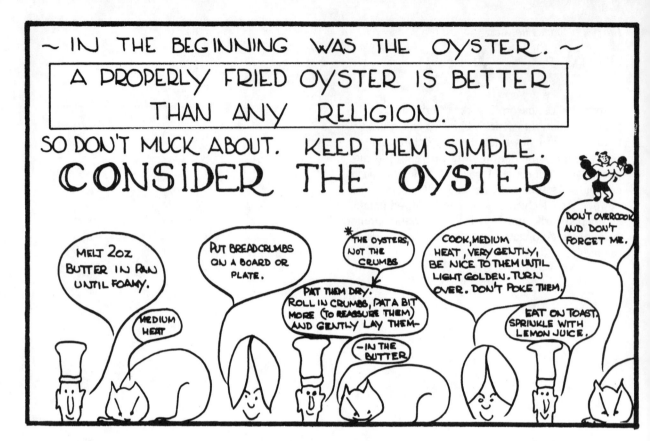

Consider the Oyster

(an homage to M.F.K. Fisher)

The less done to oysters the better. I like to sit at low tide in a big pool by a big rock at a beach on Hornby Island. With an oyster knife, a friend and a bottle of champagne. A bottle of Guiness' Stout will also do, or a good dark healthy vitamin-packed beer of any kind. We have, before the champagne ran out, managed forty apiece, straight out of the sea, out of the shell and into paradise.

Very few restaurants are to be trusted with an oyster. They don't have time to be gentle, to carefully watch, to feel for them, to understand them. There is one marvellous oyster dish, *Huitres Prince Albert*, in a Vancouver restaurant called Le Napoleon, and they manage to retain the texture and the taste of the sea, but that kind of treatment is rare.

And now you can do it. When we did this on television I received over 2,000 letters. The nicest one said "Sir, you are wicked. I love you." See what trouble a little simplicity can get you into.

Melt 2 oz butter in a pan until foamy over medium heat. Pat oysters dry and roll in bread crumbs. Lay oysters gently in butter and cook over medium heat, very gently, until they are light golden. Turn once. Eat on toast with a sprinkle of lemon juice.

Oyster Stew

You can eat them with crushed caviar on top, you can also order them Oysters Provencale, Oysters Maréchale, Oysters Tetrazzini, Oysters Poulette, Oysters Rockefeller and Oysters Kirkpatrick. There is no end to the oyster recipes of the world. All the major coastal cuisines favour them and all seem to share the same belief that they are aphrodisiac.

Brillat Savarin figured that everything was aphrodisiac. Everything edible, that is. He called it the *sens génésique,* or the sense of the learned taste buds.

Be nice to this one. Rarely can you be kind to yourself in only five minutes.

Melt 2 oz butter in a pan. Put in 1 pt oysters and juice, 1 pt milk, 1 tsp salt and a good sprinkle pepper. Cover over medium heat until edges of oysters curl. Serve immediately with a sprinkle paprika, a dob of butter and/or a couple Tbsp cream.

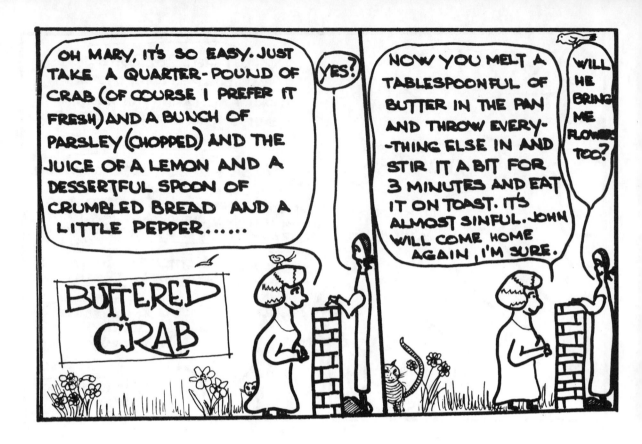

Buttered Crab

Use canned crab if you have to, but fresh is better. This is a ridiculously simple, completely foolproof recipe which is just made for bachelors, spinsters, apartment hermits and ladies who get picked up on buses and want to take him home.

This is one of the few canned meals which appeals to me. All you need to buy is a bottle of dry sherry, a couple or so of flowers and a candle, and you will have a dinner party of considerable elegance for two.

Just get things ready for the crab, shove it in the fridge and forget it. Let him, her, or whatever your fancy is, pour a glass of sherry and relax. Open a can of consommé (you may hide out in the bathroom and do it if you want to be thought really clever), dilute it with three quarters of the water recommended, and heat it. While it's heating let the hot tap run on two mugs, or cups or whatever you want to serve your consommé in. As soon as the soup is hot, pour it into the mugs and quickly dump in an ounce or two of sherry. And if you want to be elegant, float a thin slice of lemon. That's it. Stage One over.

Now do the crab. Just like the picture. If there is fresh asparagus in the stores, cook it seven minutes with a squeeze of lemon over the heads, and serve with melted butter. But if there isn't any fresh, use canned asparagus. Put it in the refrigerator for a bit, open it, drain it, and serve it cold with melted butter poured over it. Just like that.

Saturday lunch, midnight supper, after a movie, when your mother-in-law arrives, somebody special, or if you just plain want to make a pig of yourself on crab.

Combine ¼ lb crab meat, 1 small bunch chopped parsley, juice of 1 lemon, a generous tsp of bread crumbs and a bit of pepper. Melt 1 Tbsp butter in pan and add all ingredients at once. Cook, stirring, for 3 minutes. Serve on toast.

Danish Scallops

The offering of compassion, like rewards (and punishment) should be immediate. You mustn't make people wait too long when they are in need. And that includes yourself.

If someone is around to massage your eyebrows (there is nothing more gentling), and maybe to put fresh cut slices of ginger to your temples, they may also be inclined, or persuaded, to let their fingers discover the line of your jawbone beneath your skin, to hold (again very gently, try it on yourself) the bridge of your nose between thumb and fore-finger, or just to hold your head quietly between their hands. They won't really cure anything, but it's a lot better than lying on the bed looking at the ceiling and wishing you were dead.

If you want to practise being sad, and learn how it feels to have all those gentle massages taking place inside instead of outside, then this way of doing scallops is a good beginning. A discreet and gentle use of curry; the spiciness is there as a pleasant reminder of things to come.

Beat together 1 egg yolk, 2 oz cream, 1 tsp salt and ½ tsp pepper. Melt 2 oz butter over medium heat. Slice ½ lb scallops crosswise ½-inch thick. Cook scallops for 2 minutes in melted butter over low heat. Move scallops to a warm plate. Sprinkle ½ tsp curry powder in pan and cook gently, stir-ring, for 1 minute. Add ½ c white wine, boil vigorously and add 4 oz cream. Reduce heat to low and add 1 Tbsp pan mixture to egg and cream mixture, stir, then add the rest of the pan mixture, one tablespoon at a time, stirring between addi-tions. Pour liquid into the pan, stirring constantly. Immediately add scallops and cook 2 minutes over low heat. Serve with rice.

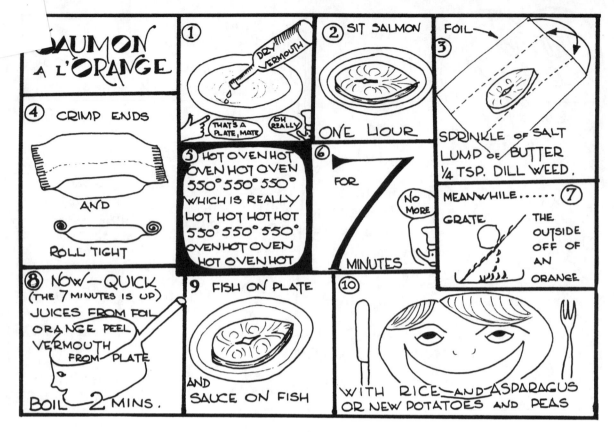

Saumon à l'Orange

This has to be one of the easiest and most pleasant ways to cook salmon. There's not even a cooking pan to wash.

Get salmon as thick as you can and as fresh as you can. And get a good dry vermouth. (I use Cazapras.) And remember that this fish is intended to be undercooked. Reduce the cooking time each time you do it, and see how much nicer undercooked fish is. And get the oven hot. Really hot.

Now, come home with the fish, put it to marinate in the vermouth (use enough—don't float it but let it soak in). That's all you do, just put it in a plate and forget it. And if you haven't yet discovered dry vermouth on the rocks now is the time. A glass, two ice cubes, two or three ounces of vermouth, and a slice of squeezed lemon peel. Sit down. Forget it. Dinner will be one hour and seven mintues. Talk to him, or her. Put your feet up, and if anybody asks you to do anything tell them you're busy—cooking dinner.

You can put the rice on half an hour before the fish is ready. Throw a few dried onion flakes in for a change, and a good knob of butter, or some fine chopped green onions, or some peas five minutes

before it's cooked. Or put turmeric with it to make it pretty. This salmon needs something more than just rice. By this time you need some more vermouth in your glass, while you turn the salmon. Turn it a couple of times during the hour. That's not too hard, is it?

When you're ready, put each salmon steak on a sheet of foil. Sprinkle salt, quite a lot of dill and a big lump of butter. Now wrap it up. Get the edges all together and crimped and rolled over. Make it tight. And put it in the oven. If the oven is hot enough, no steak needs more than seven minutes. I have cooked whole fishes (five pounds) in less than twenty. Put it in, shut the oven door, and tip the vermouth from the marinade into a heavy saucepan. Grate, for each two people, the outer, coloured skin of an orange. Which, you may be delighted to know, is called the "zest." Make sure the orange peel is fine. If your grater is very coarse, then chop it a bit before using. Put it in the pan with the vermouth, and immediately when the seven minutes are up pull out the packets of fish (use a glove), open one end of each, and pour the juices

continued

into the pan. Boil it on high heat for a minute or two. It will reduce quite noticeably. Meanwhile you are putting rice and things on plates, opening the packets of fish and looking smug.

Pour the sauce over the fish, and eat it.

Marinate salmon steak in dry vermouth for 1 hour. Reserve marinade. Wrap steak in foil with salt, lump of butter and ¼ tsp dill weed. Bake in a hot, 550 degree oven for 7 minutes. Meanwhile grate peel of 1 orange. After 7 minutes combine juice from salmon, orange peel and marinade in pan and boil 2 minutes. Sauce fish and serve.

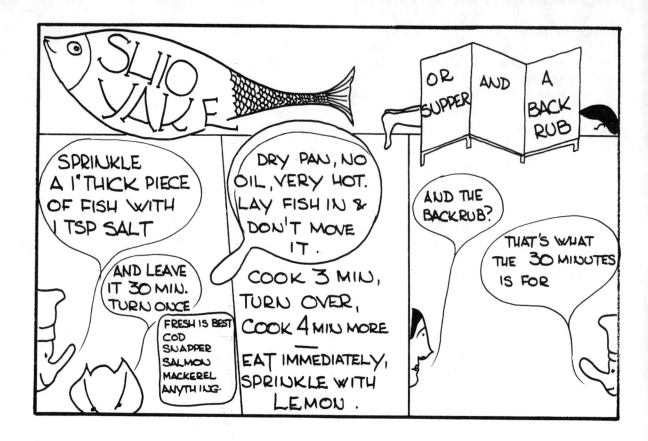

Shio Yake

Shio Yaki. (I spelled it wrong in the drawing but the drawing looked so nice!)

Salt has a bad reputation.

Lot's wife got turned into a pillar of it, which in those days, salt being so rare, must have made a wealthy man of Lot, a fact that Genesis omits to mention.

Shio Yaki is essentially Japanese cooking. It is a good summer dish for the long hot sweaty days, and salt on its own (no other seasonings) is a flavour all too seldom appreciated. Don't shove it about in the pan; let it form a glaze.

Sprinkle a 1-inch thick piece of fish with 1 tsp salt and leave it for 30 minutes, turning once. Place fish in a very hot dry pan, and cook 3 minutes. Turn fish over and cook 4 minutes more. Serve immediately with lemon.

Matelote de Fevrier

Good bread, a good dry white wine (I particularly like Vinho Verde, the Portuguese green one that tastes as though with a little encouragement it could turn into champagne) and a good leafy green salad.

In France they make this with cognac; I prefer rye. Bourbon is good too. You need a big pot, it helps if your friends help, it's quick and it's easy so you only manage one drink while it's cooking and there's some left for afterwards, when the talking starts. Whiskey first, wine with the dinner, and more whiskey for when you get your feet up on the table.

Cook 1 finely chopped onion in 2 oz melted butter over low heat for 5 minutes. Cut 2 lbs white fish into 1½-inch pieces and put in pan. Turn fish gently and add 1 lb mushrooms, halved, 1 oz rye whiskey, two anchovy fillets, cut fine, and 1 c white wine. Simmer slowly 6 minutes. Move fish to a heated plate with a slotted spoon. Turn heat to high, add 1 tsp thyme and reduce liquid to half. Add ½ c sour cream and 2 Tbsp soy sauce. Stir well. Pour over fish and serve immediately.

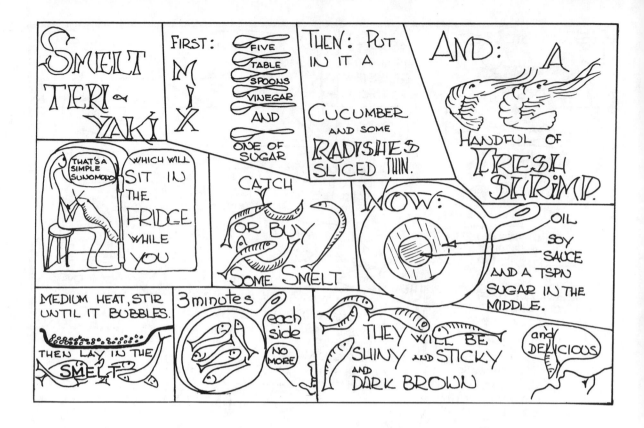

Smelt Teriyaki

On all the shores of North America, in the summer and at midnight, there are men and boys catching, one way or another, smelt. Sometimes they dip nets on poles, sometimes they hang nets in the water at the turn of the tide, sometimes they wade in with lanterns. They all have different tricks, and they all catch fish, and they all take them home in a bucket to cook.

All except those who take them to the fishmonger, who sells them, usually cheap. You can fry them dipped in flour, or make them very pompous dipped in egg and breadcrumbs, or you can try this recipe, which is so delicious that you will never try any of the others.

Don't clean them; just wipe them, lay them in the pan, heads on and all, and cook them whole. Turn them carefully—they will be a burnished coppery colour where they have been fried—and eat them like you play a mouth organ, using your front teeth the way they were designed for, nibbling the flesh off the bone like a mouthful of midnight ear. Very nice.

Fry anything in the same mixture of oil and soya sauce and sugar. The Japanese call it Teriyaki.

And of course, you take the stuff out of the fridge and eat. It's called Sunomono.

Mix 5 Tbsp vinegar and 1 Tbsp sugar. Slice thin 1 cucumber and radishes, and combine with vinegar mixture. Add 1 handful of fresh shrimp and let sit in refrigerator.

Combine oil, soy sauce and 1 tsp sugar in a pan (see illustration) and stir until it bubbles. Add smelt and cook 3 minutes on each side over medium heat.

Fish Again

There is an art to the proper mashing of potatoes. A big dollop of butter, and lots of pepper. Nothing else, no milk, no cream, just you, the potatoes and a fork.

It's tough on the wrist, unless you are a championship grade arm-wrestler or maybe a bass player in a rock group, but the end product is fluffy and light, nothing at all like instant potatoes or machine-mashed ones.

When you cook potatoes, or rice, always make twice as much as you'll need. And mash the potatoes while they're hot. Next day you make fish cakes, or Shepherd's Pie, or you mix 'em up with an egg and fry them for breakfast.

Every time I make fish cakes I turn to the East and make my apologies (forehead to the floor, three times) to Mister Heinz for all the bad things I've said in my life about ketchup. Of course, if you want to make your own ketchup—but that's another book.

Fry 1 thinly sliced onion in 2 Tbsp butter. Add 1 lb fish, 1 cup milk, pepper to taste and ½ tsp salt. Simmer 7 minutes, turning once. Mix 1 lb cooked fish with 1 or 2 c mashed potatoes. Mix well with 1 egg and half a bunch chopped parsley. Pat egg-sized portions into ½-inch thick cakes. Flour a board and pat patties on both sides. Fry patties crisp in 2 Tbsp butter. Eat hot with ketchup.

Vegetables with Dignity, Style and Anchovies

There are no leftovers, ever.

Boil several potatoes until just tender, then drain and keep covered in the cooking pan. Fry 1 or 2 cloves chopped garlic in 1 Tbsp oil over medium-high heat. Add 1 small can of mashed anchovies, a handful chopped parsley and ½ tsp pepper. Toss potatoes with anchovy mixture. Other cooked vegetables, such as broccoli, cauliflower, green beans, spinach or cooked dry beans may be substituted for potatoes.

mrs marco polo's homecoming beef stew ~

~ take 1 lb beef stew (cut up) and toss it in a bag with 3 tbsps flour.

~ fry it all sides, medium heat, in 2 tbs oil

~ add, all at once : ½ tsp pepper, 3 tbsp soya sauce, 1 tsp aniseed and 1 tsp mustard.

~ also 3 large tomatoes (or a can) and the peel of an orange.

~ simmer it one and a half hours, lid on

what do Italians do for 1½ hours? *Sing?* *change governments?* *open a restaurant?* *get tighter pants?* *all wrong. Why you think there are so many Italians...?*

Mrs. Marco Polo's Homecoming Stew

"Marco," she said, "where have you been? Twenty-four years you're gone and I'm supposed to believe it was just a boat ride? I was *worried*. And this Chinese food story? I've seen it on the television, Marco, it doesn't take 24 years, it's *quick*. So where you been? What's her name? Can she cook? Whatsa matter, you don' like Mama's food no more? Eat, eat, mangiare, mangiare..."

The only difference between Jewish mothers and Italian mamas is that the Italian ones can be bought off cheaper. Mrs. Marco P. didn't need any more than a little soya sauce to divert her, maybe a little aniseed and the idea of using orange peel.

I first discovered this stew in Naples. She was a nice lady who had never heard of Chinese food, but somebody special must have handed it down to her, because the Chinese do almost exactly the same thing—orange peel, soya sauce and star anise.

Everybody knows about Marco Polo bringing home tomatoes and noodles to Italy, and then Catherine de Medici taking good food to France. But nobody seems to have thought of this Italian recipe that puts stew and stew together.

Toss 1 lb cubed stew beef in a bag with 3 Tbsp flour. Fry on all sides over medium heat in 2 Tbsp oil. Add all at once ½ tsp pepper, 3 Tbsp soya sauce, 1 tsp aniseed, 1 tsp mustard, 3 large cut up tomatoes OR 1 can tomatoes and the peel of an orange. Simmer for 1½ hours, covered.

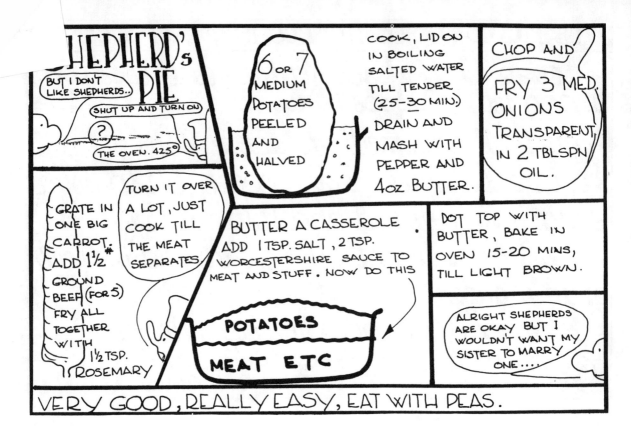

Shepherd's Pie

This is a real idiot's recipe for the completely non-cook who wants to make a start somewhere. It is impossible not to make this well, and everybody loves it—the young, the toothless and the in-betweens, the cat and the girl in the next apartment. Everybody except the dog, because there never seems to be enough left for him. It's a social dish, two plates and two forks, and it's real cooking, home cooking.

In England, it is a Wednesday dish. Hot roast on Sunday, cold on Monday (washing day), curried roast on Tuesday and what's left over, ground up, in Shepherd's pie on Wednesday. But it is much better made with fresh ground meat. It makes its own gravy, the top is crisp and brown and, if you are in a hurry or it isn't early summer when the fresh ones come, frozen peas are just great.

Try the peas this way: Two tablespoons butter in a saucepan, two tablespoons water. Half a teaspoon sugar, and a sprinkling of mint (fresh if it's available). Half a teaspoon salt. Heat, toss it about for three or four minutes.

Preheat over to 425 degrees, and peel and halve 6 or 7 potatoes. Cook potatoes, covered, in boiling salted water until tender, 25 to 30 minutes. Drain potatoes and mash with 4 oz butter and pepper. Chop and fry 3 medium onions until transparent in 2 Tbsp oil. Grate 1 large carrot into pan and add 1½ lb ground beef. Fry with 1½ tsp rosemary, turning often, until meat separates. Add 1 tsp salt and 2 tsp Worcestershire sauce to meat. Butter a casserole, fill bottom with meat mixture and cover with mashed potatoes. Dot top with butter and bake in oven 15 to 20 minutes, until light brown.

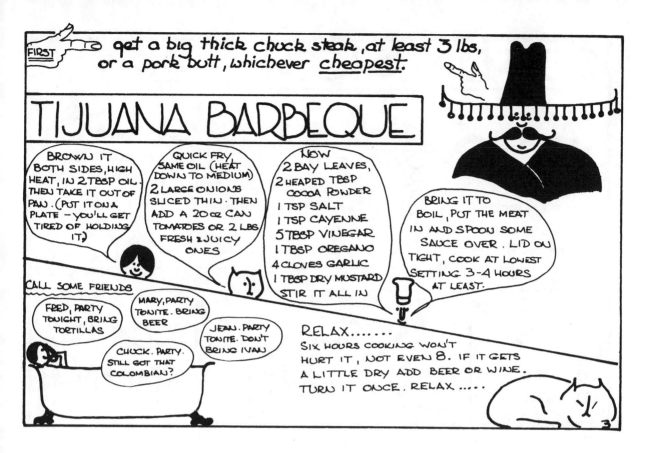

Tijuana Barbecue

Half an hour's drive from San Diego (just over ten minutes if you're a California driver), is the Mexican border. And the border is Tijuana, a city of 24-hour-a-day nightclubs, of fresh pressed fruit juices sold on the street, of poverty and wealth, of little kids with more financial acumen than a Montreal furrier, of cheap tequila, good beer, wonderful food, and, despite the popular myth, a lot of hard-working people. They work hard because they're poor and don't want to stay that way.

They like to eat, but they don't have a lot of time to cook. They don't have a lot of fancy equipment either, and they buy cheap meat because it's cheap. People go to Tijuana from Los Angeles and San Diego, and they bring back, or try to bring back, all sorts of exotic goodies.

I bring back peppers, fifteen or twenty different varieties—mild ones, musty ones, purple ones, red hot screamers, yellow ones—and they all have different uses. I also bring back memories of magnificent, cheap and flavourful meals, and spend months trying to duplicate them with what's available in my corner store.

This recipe is an adaptation of a lady called Beth's adaptation of her memory. It tastes remark-ably authentic, and it's a real reputation-maker for very little money. Cook it very, very slowly: go out to a movie, go shopping, do the laundry, just don't worry about it. The meat fibres will separate, so you can pull it apart with a fork and shovel it onto bread or tortillas. Warm it up next day with a little extra wine or water. Always cook it slowly, lick your fingers frequently and for best effect use no plates, just tortillas and a deft hand.

Brown both sides of a 3-lb chuck steak or pork butt in 2 Tbsp oil over high heat and move to a plate. Quick-fry 2 large onions sliced thin in same oil and add a 20-oz can tomatoes or 2 lbs fresh cut tomatoes. Add 2 bay leaves, 2 heaping Tbsp cocoa powder, 1 tsp salt, 1 tsp cayenne, 5 Tbsp vinegar, 1 Tbsp oregano, 4 cloves garlic and 1 Tbsp dry mustard and stir well. Bring pot to boil, put meat in and spoon sauce over it. Cover, reduce heat and simmer for 3 to 4 hours, stirring occasionally. Add beer or wine if it needs more liquid.

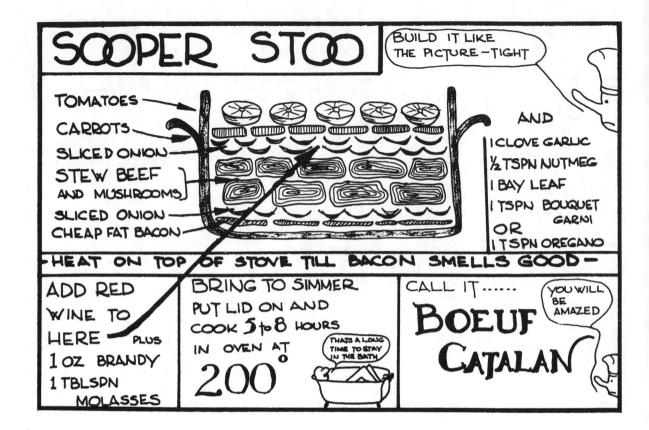

Super Stoo

Boeuf Catalan is an adaptation of a really magnificient Spanish stew. Preparation takes about fifteen minutes, after which you just leave it to cook. It is a weekend stew, something to make, put to cook, and forget about until you come home.

Just set the oven to its lowest setting, just under 200 degrees if you can, and certainly not above. The house will smell nice, and it is pleasant to come home after a movie, or skiing, or a walk in the rain.

For economy's sake, you can use dry cider instead of the wine and brandy, but the nutmeg and molasses are essential.

A pound and a half of stewing beef will feed four, the cheaper meat is hard to find. Buy bacon ends or scraps—most of today's bacon is fat anyway, and all you need in this stew is the flavour.

Cooking at this low temperature also lets you cook overnight while you sleep. Then take it out of the oven, put in the refrigerator, and reheat whenever you need it.

Reheating is best done in a 350-degree oven for twenty minutes or so—not on the top of the stove,

where the bottom will burn unless you stir it, and stirring will turn it into mush.

This way, it is an attractive dish. Another advantage of low temperature cooking is that you can use any saucepan, even one with a plastic handle, because nothing burns. The meat won't shrink, and the wine won't evaporate—you get all you bought on your plate.

After you have made it the first time, you will be a stew cook, able to go anywhere in the world and be welcome. There are as many different stews as there are cooks, and don't let anybody tell you different. Be inventive. The only rule is not to boil or overheat.

If you like your stews thicker (this one is what the French call a knife-and-fork soup) pour off most of the gravy and thicken it by stirring in a couple of tablespoons of flour smoothed in a little water. (Use a fork.) Boil it 'til it thickens, then pour it back on the stew.

Thick or thin, eat it with plain boiled potatoes and some nice people.

continued

Layer in a casserole: bacon, sliced onion, sliced mushrooms and stew beef, in chunks, sliced onion, sliced carrots and sliced tomatoes. Add 1 clove garlic, ½ tsp nutmeg, 1 bay leaf, 2 sprigs parsley and 1 tsp thyme (OR, substitute 1 tsp oregano for parsley and thyme). Heat casserole on the stove until bacon begins to cook. Add dry red wine to cover, 1 oz brandy and 1 Tbsp molasses. Bring stew back to a simmer on the stove and cook for 5 to 8 hours in a 200 degree oven (no hotter).

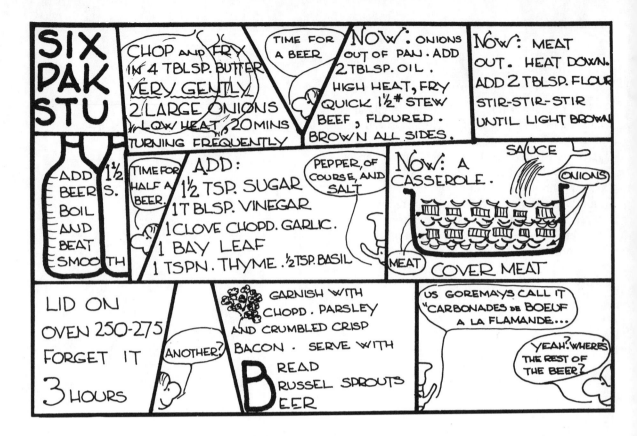

Six Pak Stu

This is a nice, thick, belly-lining stew that makes a pound and a half of meat go a long way. I like to make it on a Sunday afternoon, put it in the oven and go for a walk.

With heavy rye bread, and Brussels sprouts or braised leeks, it is a pleasantly satisfying meal with friends and a case of beer.

If you want to be elegant, and call it *Carbonades de Boeuf à la Flamande*, then feel happy about it. Light candles, put flowers on the table, get a good rough Burgundy and cook a lot of asparagus.

The only care you must take is in making the roux. That's the mixing in of the flour, after you have fried the meat. There should be sufficient fat left in the pan to cook the flour and, if you scrape around a lot and make sure that every bit of sediment gets mixed in, it will taste much better when it gets to the table. But cook the roux gently, very low heat, stirring all the time, with the fork held flat on the bottom of the pan.

Fry 2 large chopped onions in 4 Tbsp butter very gently over low heat, about 20 minutes. Take onions out of pan, add 2 Tbsp oil and brown quickly 1½ lb floured stew beef over high heat. Take meat out, add 2 Tbsp flour and stir constantly until light brown. Add 1½ bottles beer, 1½ tsp sugar, 1 Tbsp vinegar, 1 clove chopped garlic, 1 bay leaf, 1 tsp thyme and ½ tsp basil. Salt and pepper to taste. Layer onions and meat in a casserole and cover with sauce. Cover and cook in a 250 to 275 degree oven for 3 hours. See serving suggestions.

Cevapcici

There is an art to riding a donkey. A fast one travels at something less than two miles per hour if it's pointed towards home, and about half that in any other direction. A donkey is uncomfortable, uncooperative and unpredictable. Occasionally it will bite. And about 3:00 p.m. it starts looking for a place to spend the night. There is nothing you can do about it; it moves off the road and heads for any house that has a barn.

In Yugoslavia, where I first discovered donkeys, houses with barns seemed to anticipate donkeys and the people on their backs. There was always hay, and there was almost always lamb, usually a whole lamb cooking over an open fire, with a very old lady slowly turning it, basting it with oil, and sipping almost as regularly on a bottle of slivovitz.

Onion salad came with it: thin sliced raw onion with a little pepper, salt and pumpkin seed oil. Bread, of course, and red wine. It seemed to straighten you out, put the spark back in your eyes. There was always an hour or two to wait for supper, and if you were lucky, before the lamb, there would be Cevapcici (che-vap-chi-chi, if you're still wondering).

In the mountains outside Sarajevo they make Cevapcici from ground lamb. In the cities they sell them barbecued, without sauce, just chopped onions. And from house to house, like all good food, the recipe is different. This is the best we can do with what's regularly available to us, using local stuff. It's an enormous improvement on plain hamburger.

Of course if you've got a donkey, and a lamb or two, then all you need for total authenticity is an aged grandmother...

Mix ½ lb hamburger, 1 medium chopped onion with 1 clove chopped garlic, 1 egg, ½ tsp pepper, 1 large tsp oregano and 1 tsp paprika. Roll the mixture into thumb-sized bits, roll them in flour, and fry in 2 Tbsp oil over medium-high heat. When meat is brown add 1 chopped tomato, ½ tsp salt and ⅓ bottle of beer, tossing well. Simmer 5 minutes and serve with rice or noodles.

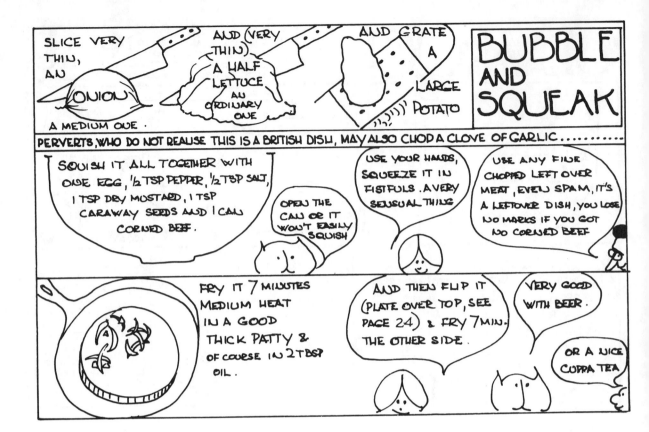

Bubble and Squeak

British children learn at their mothers' knees to cook cabbage. Not just to cook it, but to destroy it—to give it a terrible reputation and make an international joke of it. But out of this soggy, tasteless mess they also learn to make a most magnificent dish called Bubble and Squeak, which when properly made is as close as the British will ever come to Soul Food.

To make an authentic Bubble and Squeak requires lamb left over from the Sunday roast and cold cooked potatoes from the same meal. Also quantities of leftover cooked cabbage, and that it be Monday, and that it be cooked by a Mum.

You won't find Bubble and Squeak in pubs because it's not a dish that lends itself to mass production. It's a dish I remember fondly from my childhood, and for years I knocked on the doors of British expatriates (always on Mondays) hoping that they would say apologetically, "There's only Bubble and Squeak"...but it seems to be a lower-class dish and therefore shameful—the sort of thing people eat in private.

So we had to develop a recipe for ourselves, using ingredients more readily available. This one tastes remarkably like the original: crusty on the outside, squishy in the middle. We frequently cook it on the boat where space, ingredients and time are always at a minimum.

Sliver very thin 1 onion and ½ head of firmly packed lettuce. Grate 1 large potato. Mix ingredients with 1 egg, ½ tsp pepper, ½ tsp salt, 1 tsp dry mustard, 1 tsp caraway seeds and 1 can corned beef or other leftover meat. Squeeze mixture well with your hands and fry it in a cake over medium heat for 7 minutes in 2 Tbsp oil. Turn and fry other side for 7 minutes.

Faggots

There are people who would have you call these Faggots *Frikadellen,* or even *Kuzu Ciger Colmasi,* and have you scurrying all over town looking for a copper pan *exactly* 2.75 centimetres deep. Faggots are basic working class food the world over, and in England, particularly in the north, they preceded the most famous of British folk foods, fish and chips.

Faggots and chips—we used to get them after a movie. There are still not as many cars in England as in North America, and making out in the back seat is the exception rather than the rule. After a movie in such outposts of Empire as Nottingham, one announced the seriousness of one's intentions by suggesting first: "Wanna walk a bit?" and second: " 'Ow about some faggots?"

There were those who took their newspaper-wrapped packets unashamedly to the river bank, but another school firmly convinced that horizontal sex was not nice repaired to dark shop doorways where they would consume their Faggots and chips over one another's shoulders...

Standing up, sitting down, off a plate or out of a newspaper, at cocktail parties or kids' dinners, they are simple, cheap, and I've never met anybody who didn't like them.

Mix 1 c bread crumbs, 1 tsp salt, 1 tsp pepper, 2 tsp thyme, 1 c chopped parsley, ½ lb ground beef and 1 medium onion chopped fine. Mix in ½ lb of liver and ½ c chopped mushrooms (optional). Flatten tablespoonfuls of the mixture to about ½-inch thick and press into bread crumbs. Fry in 2 Tbsp oil at medium heat until they are dark, nutty brown, about 3 minutes each side. Serve with Worchestershire sauce.

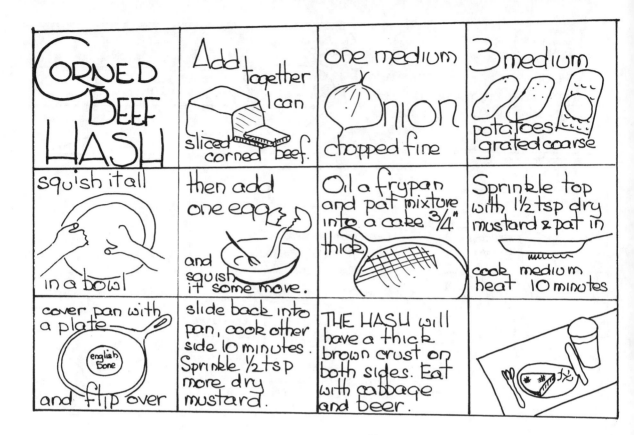

Corned Beef Hash

Forty years ago, I learned to cook corned beef hash in a mess kit over an open fire, in a field under an apple tree. With a girl. The army gave us the corned beef, we stole the onions and potatoes from a farm, and she brought some bacon fat to cook with.

Nowadays I am a little more sophisticated about it but the flavour is still there—the crisp, almost-burned outside and the squishy, steaming inside. Kids like it, and they particularly like their fathers to make it. Wives like it, people on boats like it, it's great on beaches and just as good in the kitchen on a Sunday afternoon.

And it's easy. And cheap.

I use canned corned beef. Slice the onions thin and chop them into half-inch strips. Slice the corned beef and put it in a bowl with the onions, a little more pepper than you think you should use, and a level teaspoonful of salt. Get your fingers in it, squish it about until it's well mixed, then throw in an egg.

Squish it some more with the potatoes. Some people use a fork at this stage, but fingers are better.

Put a litttle oil, or bacon fat, or butter, in the frying pan (preferably a heavy one), heat it just to smoking, and spread the mixture about half an inch thick—or three-quarters, depending on how crispy you like the outside.

Sprinkle the top with mustard powder, about a teaspoonful or a bit more, and spread it with a knife or your fingers. Cook it on a medium fire until it slides readily in the pan, when the bottom will have a well-baked crust. About ten minutes.

Now comes the trick. Put a large plate over the pan, hold it steady, and turn the whole thing over. The crisp side is now topside up on the plate. Put the pan back on the fire, add a little more fat, and slide the whole thing gently but quickly back and forth for another ten minutes. Sprinkle and pat more mustard onto the top (the crispy side), while it's cooking, and when it's done slide the whole thing out onto a plate.

Good with cabbage. Slice the cabbage thin, cut out the core, and place in a heavy saucepan with a couple of tablespoons of oil, a tablespoonful of

continued

water, half a teaspoonful of salt, and a good
sprinkling of pepper. Don't be scared of the pepper. Put the lid on, cook over medium heat, shaking frequently—about ten minutes, until it's just
cooked, just transparent.

Combine sliced corn beef, 1 finely chopped
onion and 8 coarsely grated potatoes. Add one egg
and stir to mix. Make ½- to ¾-inch cakes, sprinkle
with 1½ tsp dry mustard and cook over medium
heat for 10 minutes. Turn, add ½ tsp hot mustard
and cook another 10 minutes, or until hash has a
thick brown crust on both sides.

McDonald's Hamburger

One day all the meat in North America will be trucked to Chicago and poked down a big hole, under which is a thirty-six zillion horsepower blender.

The meat will all be ground to the same squished bland tastelessness as cat food and then pumped, in stainless steel pipes, to every street corner in the world, where, if you put a dollar in a slot, a bun will drop down and splat—there's your hamburger.

To stave off that evil day.....

Combine in a bowl 1 egg, ½ lb ground beef, ½ tsp nutmeg, ½ tsp aniseed, ½ onion, chopped fine, ½ tsp salt and ½ tsp pepper. Pat into 1-inch thick patties on a well floured board. Fry 4 minutes each side over low-medium heat.

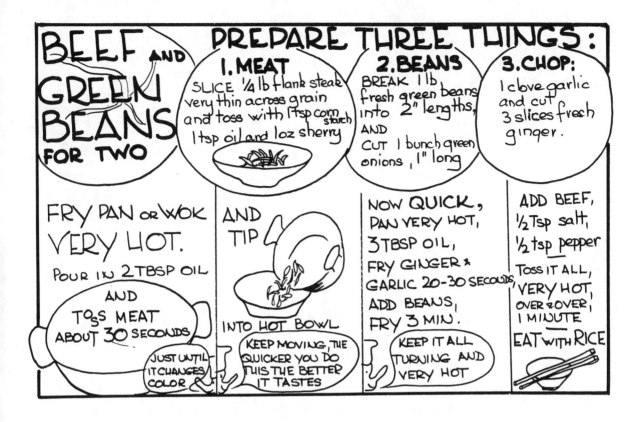

Beef and Green Beans for Two

If you can learn to do this properly, which means quickly, you will have mastered the first technique of Chinese cooking, without having to buy a wok, or taking a course at night school, or spending five years learning the 224 primitive elements of the ancient Chinese characters.

Basically this is "stir-frying," and it means getting everything ready first, the rice cooked, the meat cut, everything right there, and the people with their tongues hanging out. Chinese food is nothing you keep hot; the guests have to wait for it, not the other way round.

But they don't have to wait long. I can have dinner on the table fourteen minutes after I get in the door, and it would be sooner if the rice didn't take exactly that long to cook.

And the really great thing about it is that you feel like such a cook. It's magic—dinner seems to come straight out of the shopping bag. And it's cheap—how else can a quarter pound of meat feed two people? But do remember, this is a dish for two. Don't get ambitious and make it for your in-laws, your best beloved's sister, her room-mate and a couple people from the office. That way lies disaster.

Slice ¼ lb flank steak very thin across grain and toss with 1 tsp cornstarch, 1 tsp oil and 1 oz sherry. Break 1 lb fresh green beans into 2-inch lengths. Cut 1 bunch green onions 1 inch long. Chop 1 clove garlic and cut 3 slices fresh ginger. Heat 2 Tbsp oil very hot in a fry pan or wok. Toss meat in oil for 30 seconds and tip into a hot bowl. Heat 3 Tbsp oil very hot, quick fry ginger and garlic 20 to 30 seconds, add beans and fry 3 minutes. Add beef, ½ tsp salt, ¼ tsp pepper and toss it all 1 minute. Serve with rice.

Stifado

Buy whole cloves because the powdered ones lose the oil which makes the taste. One clove between the gum and an aching tooth will see you through until the dentist gets back from the golf course; two cloves transform even the most commonplace of curry powders; three in applesauce, the same in rhubarb; a few in stewed plums, in mulled wine, in hot beer drinks, in tea, in lemonade, in marinades; stuck in ham, of course; stuck in onions that are going into a stew (particularly good with oxtail), and in this very comforting Greek stew—Stifado.

And if you want to do something particularly nice for a Christmas present, buy a couple of jars of cloves and seek out the roundest, most perfect, medium-size orange in the market. Poke a hole through the skin with a toothpick, then stick in a clove. And another and another, all the way round its waist in a straight line, as close as you can get them to one another. Another line above the first, one below, and so on, until the whole orange bristles with cloves. The Elizabethans called them pomanders and carried them about believing that the sweet aromas would protect them against infec-

tion. Nowadays people put them in their underwear drawers, and they're supposed to last as long as love is true. I once flew from Vancouver to New York to spend Christmas with my true love and spent the whole trip making her a pomander. The airplane was filled with a wonderful smell, and when I got to her apartment her roommate told me sorry but she'd gone to Puerto Rico with a computer programmer. The pomander didn't explode, so I gave it to the roommate. We had a good Christmas.

Fry lamb or beef, cubed, in 2 Tbsp hot oil for 2 or 3 minutes over high heat. Meanwhile slice thin an onion and cook it in the same pan, pushing the meat aside. Add 8 cloves, 1 tsp salt, ½ tsp cinnamon, ½ tsp pepper, 1 whole unpeeled clove garlic and 1 can tomatoes. Cover, reduce heat and simmer for 3 hours. Drop 10 or 12 small onions in boiling water for 2 minutes, then rub off skins and add to pan. Simmer for another 45 minutes.

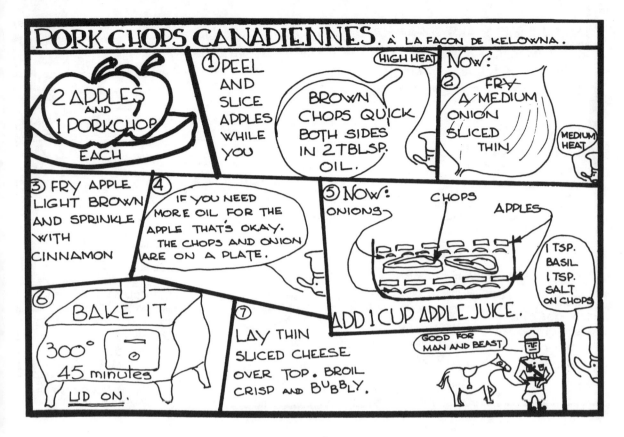

Pork Chops Canadiennes à la Façon de Kelowna

It smells so nice. Like an old French kitchen with a pot on the stove. I learned to cook with apple juice in Normandy, where the apple is a large and important part of the farm economy. They make cider from it, and a most lethal drink called Calvados. The girls use it for their complexions (and there is nothing like an armful of girl smelling of fresh pressed apples), the pigs eat a lot of them, and in fall the pork takes on a very interesting colour and flavour.

There are not many apple-fed pigs in North America, but if you want to get the special flavour, here it is, sort of sweet, a little spicy from the cinnamon, and very tender. I eat it with heavy rye bread and asparagus when it's in season. *Bon appétit.*

Peel and slice 2 apples for each person. Meanwhile brown 1 pork chop for each person in 2 Tbsp oil over high heat. Fry 1 thinly sliced onion over medium heat. Remove onion and chops and add more oil, if necessary. Fry apple until light brown and sprinkle with cinnamon. Layer in a casserole the onion, apples and meat; add 1 tsp basil, 1 tsp salt, 1 c apple juice. Bake, covered, in a 300 degree oven for 45 minutes. Lay thin slices cheese over top and broil until brown and bubbly.

Immanuel Kant's Famous 2 Pork Chops, Some Celery and 2 Big Old Carrots Recipe

Pimps, dope dealers, writers, drunks and neurotics head most parents' lists of people their kids should not get mixed up with, along with actors, gays, Marxists, bikers, environmentalists and chicken egg sexers.

But nobody worries about philosophers. And the universities are turning them out almost as fast as McDonald's is making hamburgers—nice healthy ordinary-looking people, who can be discovered washing dishes, digging ditches, selling sofas in department stores, babysitting, dog-walking, washing cars, sweeping the floors of newspaper offices and (the luckiest and least offensive of them) sitting soulfully behind the counter of small bookstores, reading themselves into functional blindness. They like to eat, although they are not concerned with the process any more than a car cares about which gas pump.

They also like to talk. And talk and talk and talk. If you should find yourself involved with philosophers, the trick is to find them something simple to do while they are talking. Sit them in a chair, or prop them up against the kitchen counter, give them simple and unequivocal instructions (otherwise they are likely to get involved in the semantics of seasonings) and keep them moving.

If they insist that you become involved in their conversations, long words are not necessary. "Possibly," or "But on the other hand," with a little doubt thrown in for luck, or even the carefully timed raising of eyebrows, all are sufficient to set them off for another fifteen minutes.

Slice carrots ½-inch thick and fry in 2 Tbsp very hot oil. Turn carrots and move to side of pan. Put chops in pan and brown for 2 minutes on high heat. Add 1 sliced medium onion, stirring so it won't stick. Cut 6 stalks celery in half, toss with onion in oil, add ½ a lemon, ½ c stock OR wine, ½ tsp salt and plenty of pepper. Simmer 25 minutes.

Pork Chops, mit Sort of Sauerkraut

Gourmet doesn't have to be wine. Sure, it's fine, those sauces of such elegance, and you can even make this with white wine if you want to. It won't taste the same—it will be different and it will be good, just as it will if you make it with chicken stock. But you don't have to have a Ph.D. in cork sniffing to be a good cook. The big test is the look on people's faces, and how much is left in the dish.

This is a fine friendly supper for two, preferably two amiable, beer drinking, nicely tired people who have spent a good day together and don't want to wait too long before they spend a good night together.

We invented it one day in Degnen Bay after seven hours with the wind up our nose, victims of a schedule, sailing across the Strait of Georgia when we should have stayed tied to the wharf and in bed. She tidied the deck and lit the lamps, I cooked down below where it wasn't raining.

But it works equally well in a Montreal garret.

Brown 2 pork chops in 2 Tbsp very hot oil. Meanwhile slice thin 1 small cabbage and 2 onions. Put chops to side of pan and fry onions over high heat. Add cabbage and toss over high heat until it is shiny and coated. Add a lot of pepper, 1 tsp salt and 2 tsp caraway OR aniseed. Add ½ bottle of beer and 2 oz vinegar. Slice 2 potatoes ¼-inch thick. Put the chops on the cabbage, spread potatoes over top and sprinkle with ½ tsp salt. Cover and simmer over low heat for 15 minutes. Eat with rye bread and mustard.

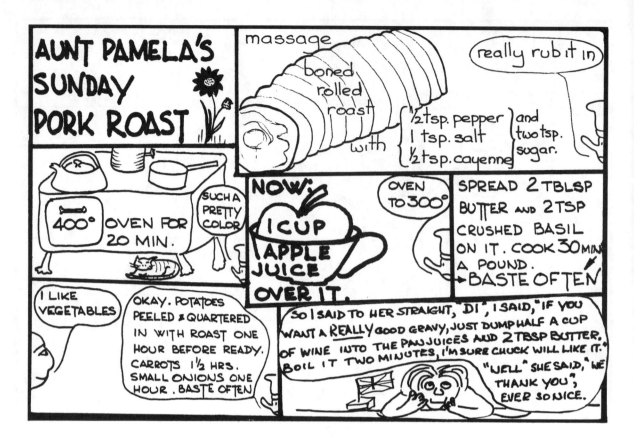

Aunt Pamela's Sunday Pork Roast

Aunt Pamela is not really very nice at all. She is a garrulous old windbag who has talked three husbands to death. But she can cook. That's how she catches them. She does this on Sundays in spring, when pork is cheap. She spends the afternoon looking smug, nipping in and out of the kitchen in her apron, and suddenly everything is ready, all on one dish. She talks and everybody else eats. It's very good. A five pound roast will feed about twelve people. Or four teenagers.

If you get organized first, peel the potatoes and quarter them, peel the onions and cut the carrots so they are all about as thick as your thumb. There's nothing to do for the rest of the afternoon except smell it cooking. After the first twenty minutes it is a nice cinnamon colour, and it gets darker and darker until it's ready. You can use zucchini instead of carrots, or leeks, or celery. But keep the onions, they're nice.

And if you have any spare room in the oven, put a couple of apples apiece in a baking dish. Don't peel them, just cut out the cores and fill them with brown sugar and raisins. Push it in with your thumb, and heap it on top. Put a little water in the pan and bake them for an hour, basting occasionally. Very good with ice cream. And a little cinnamon in the sugar is good. Pour the juice over it all.

And the meat gravy. No flour, just a little stock, scrape well around the bottom of the pan and mix it well while it boils down. Happy Sunday.

Rub boned rolled pork roast with ½ tsp pepper, 1 tsp salt, ½ tsp cayenne and 2 tsp sugar. Brown roast in a preheated 400 degree oven for 20 minutes. Pour 1 c apple juice over roast and turn down heat to 300 degrees. Spread 2 Tbsp butter and 2 tsp basil on roast and cook 30 minutes per pound, basting often. One and a half hours before serving add peeled and quartered carrots; 1 hour before serving add peeled and quartered potatoes and small onions. Remove meat and vegetables. Add ½ c stock and 2 Tbsp butter to pan juices and boil two minutes. Pour over roast and serve.

The Ultimate Simplicity

Every Wednesday night in the logging camp we got sausage and cabbage. The cook said it was a Ukrainian dish. He was Chinese. The other nights we got chicken and steak and pork chops, but Wednesday night was the one we looked forward to.

A great supper for poker nights, the day before payday, Grey Cup parties. And kids like it too.

Cut smoked meat into 1-inch pieces and a white cabbage into ¼-inch slices. Toss cabbage and lots of pepper in 2 Tbsp hot butter for 2 minutes. Add sausage and an egg cup of water, toss and simmer, covered tight, for 20 minutes.

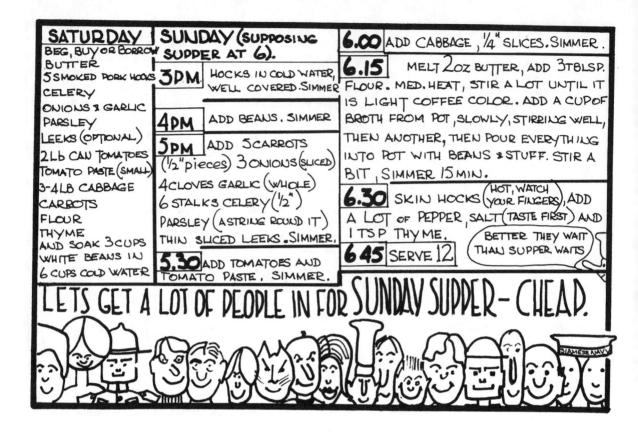

Sunday Supper Cheap

If you want to be extravagant and find a goose or a duck to put in this, then you have the beginnings of a magnificent dish called cassoulet, a very famous dish from Toulouse, where France's most famous cooks all seem to have their restaurants.

Beans are a specialty of Toulouse, and it seems fitting that in the town there is also a very famous music school.

But we are not talking about cassoulet, which takes forty-eight hours to prepare. This is very close to it, a wonderful cold winter night supper to let you all pretend you have come in from the back forty to thaw out your noses.

The pork hocks are usually the cheapest thing in the butcher shop, but you can add smoked sausage if you like, or (most marvellous) smoked pork loin, which the delicatessens call Kassler. And if you want more meat than the pork hocks offer, a picnic ham is fine. It's one of those infinitely expandable, non-stopwatch, nice and relaxed, stir it occasionally, sit around and talk, eat it off Salvation Army plates suppers that needs a loaf of really good bread to go with it, any kind of booze at all, and some fresh fruit for dessert.

Best of all, it's the kind of supper that makes people react quite happily to the suggestion that they wash their own dishes.

Have on hand the ingredients listed above. Soak 3 c white beans in 6 c cold water overnight. About 4 hours before serving, cover 5 smoked pork hocks in cold water and simmer. Three hours before serving, add soaked beans and continue simmering. Two hours before serving, add 5 carrots cut in ½-inch pieces, 3 sliced onions, 4 whole cloves garlic, 6 stalks celery cut in ½-inch pieces, a bundle of parsley and some sliced leeks (optional). About 1½ hours before serving, add a 2 lb can of tomatoes and 1 small can tomato paste, and simmer. Forty-five minutes before serving add 1 3- or 4-lb cabbage sliced ¼-inch thick. Half an hour before serving melt 2 oz butter, add 3 Tbsp flour and stir over medium heat until it turns brown. Add 1 c broth from pot slowly, stirring well, then add another c broth. Pour mixture into pot with beans and meat. Stir, reduce heat and simmer 15 minutes. Before serving, skin hocks, add plenty of pepper, salt to taste and 1 tsp thyme. Serves 12.

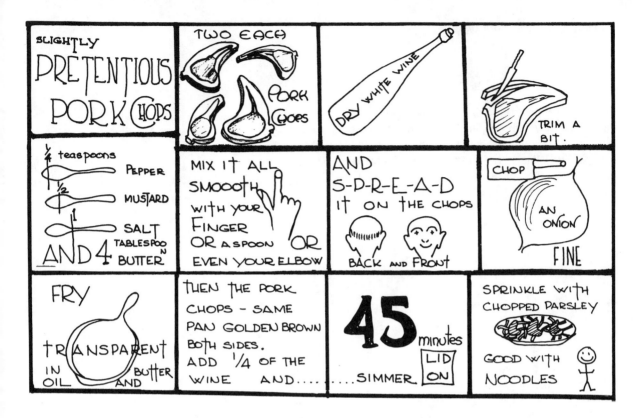

Slightly Pretentious Pork Chops

When you are in a hurry is no time to eat. This is a very simple, very easy and very satisfying dish that gives you at least half an hour to sit and reflect upon the injustices the world has this day wrought upon you. It is another frying pan dish, which needs a lid.

The ingredients are in most corner stores, so, even at midnight, if you want to cook, you can do it—if you have wine.

And, if you haven't, use apple juice. It will taste different. Not better, not worse (there are no absolutes in the vocabulary of a good cook) but just different.

Fresh pork is best but, even if the only chops you can get are frozen, no matter—do just as the recipe says. But rub the paste well in with your fingers. Really rub it in. Don't lick your fingers—the sauce is pretty fierce until it is cooked.

If you like the pork and mustard flavour, you might like to try something really pretentious, which is almost as easy. It is called Pork Chops a l'Auberge du Grand Saint Pierre and involves the same pork chops, trimmed the same, and then gently fried (medium heat) in oil and butter, after

rubbing in a little pepper and salt.

Now make a paste of finely grated Gruyère cheese (about a quarter of a pound), two teaspoonfuls of mustard and enough whipping cream to make it all smooth. Spread it thickly on the chops, and put it under the broiler until the sauce is golden.

And, if you want to be Portuguese, or pretty close, sauté the outside of the chops, and dump a can of tomatoes and a bay leaf in the pan with them.

Let it all happen, then maybe some oregano and a little sherry, for about an hour. And, if you are going to be really Portuguese, leave all the fat on. Don't trim it at all.

This dish, with tomatoes, is almost infinitely expandable so that, if the smell leaks down the hall, and your friends stop by, just throw in some potatoes and another onion, and a bit more pepper and salt, and another bay leaf. If you haven't trimmed the pork, there will be flavour enough for ten.

continued

Trim fat from 2 pork chops for each person. Mix until smooth ¼ tsp pepper, ½ tsp mustard, 1 tsp salt and 4 Tbsp butter. Spread sauce on both sides chops. Fry 1 finely chopped onion until transparent in oil and butter. Brown pork chops in same oil, add ¼ bottle wine and simmer, covered, 45 minutes.

Chinese FOOD IN 5 MINUTES

4 strips fat bacon, chopped up.

1 clove garlic, peeled and chopped (garlic presses are a waste of time)

1 inch fresh ginger sliced thin AND half an onion sliced thick.

AND/OR celery green beans green onion bok choy. all sliced coarse

NOW: high heat.
1. the bacon until transparent.
2. the ginger.

3. the garlic.
4. the onion
5. anything else
6. ½ tsp salt.
7 ½ tsp. pepper

STIR IT CONTINUOUSLY 2 minutes.

Add: ½ lb bean sprouts and mix in.

☆ Cook 2 min, lid on.
☆ Mix 1 tsp cornstarch in sherry or water, stir in to pan.

Eat with chopsticks or a fork, rice and a smug content.

Chinese Food in Five Minutes

Stir frying is a basic technique of Chinese cooking. It is a quick, easy and energetic method that requires your complete attention for five minutes and is something well worth learning. The food is bright and attractive, better than you get in all but the best Chinese restaurants and as economical or extravagent as you wish to make it.

The first time I suggest that you start with very simple ingredients. Bean sprouts, green pepper, a couple sticks of celery, and either green beans or bok choy (that's the Chinese cabbage with thick white stems). Get a little of each. Bean sprouts are in the supermarket in packets or loose in Chinatown. A handful of beans, a quarter pound of mushrooms and a bunch of green onions will do it. Root ginger—not powdered—is the only kind for getting the right taste. Garlic, powdered if you must, but it's much better to learn about it fresh. Just crush a clove with the side of a knife and the skin will shake off. Then chop it fine.

First, put on the rice, one cup rice, two cups water, a pinch of salt, bring to a boil, stir once, put lid on tight and turn the heat down to the lowest you can. No peeking, just leave it for twenty minutes. While it's cooking, cut the vegetables.

Celery, green beans in one-inch lengths. Little mushrooms halved, big ones sliced. Bok choy in one-inch lengths. Green onions in one-inch lengths, but separate the white part and the green. Cut an onion into coarse pieces (about one inch).

If you haven't got a wok then use a heavy frying pan, fairly big. If you haven't got a heavy frying pan, make up your mind to get one. You're going to need it if you like my cooking. Start when the rice has been on for fifteen minutes.

Cut three or four strips of fat bacon into quarter inch slices. Or use bacon ends which are cheaper. Or hog jowl which is even cheaper. Fry it with the garlic until transparent. Grate in about a quarter inch of the ginger root (don't peel it, just grate it on the coarse grater).

The pan will be hot and on the point of smoking. Keep it hot, dump in the celery and turn it over and over (from underneath) in the fat. Thirty seconds later put in the bok choy, beans, the onion and green pepper.

continued

Keep turning it over. Don't mess about from the top, get under it. Coat everything with the bacon fat and keep it moving. Use a pancake turner or anything else big.

Thirty seconds later, put in the bean sprouts. Pepper, a good pinch of salt, keep turning over and over, pan very hot. Now the mushrooms, and the green onions (the white part). Lid on the pan (it will be ready in two minutes).

A teaspoonful of cornstarch dissolved in a little water, a soup cube in half a cup of hot water. Take off the lid one minute before it's ready, put in the soup stock and green parts of the onions. Turn it all. Put in the cornstarch. Turn it all. Cook thirty seconds. Take it off the stove into a dish, eat on rice. Good with beer.

In a heavy fry pan or wok fry 4 strips chopped fat bacon. Add 1 crushed garlic clove, ½-inch piece ginger root and ½ coarsely chopped onion. Cook over high heat for 30 seconds. Add any combination of chopped celery, beans, green pepper, bok choy, green onions and mushrooms. Cook over high heat, turning constantly for another 30 seconds. Add ½ lb bean sprouts and salt and pepper to taste. Cover and cook 2 minutes. Add 1 soup cube dissolved in ½ c sherry OR water and 1 tsp cornstarch dissolved in a little hot water, cooking for 1 minute after each addition.

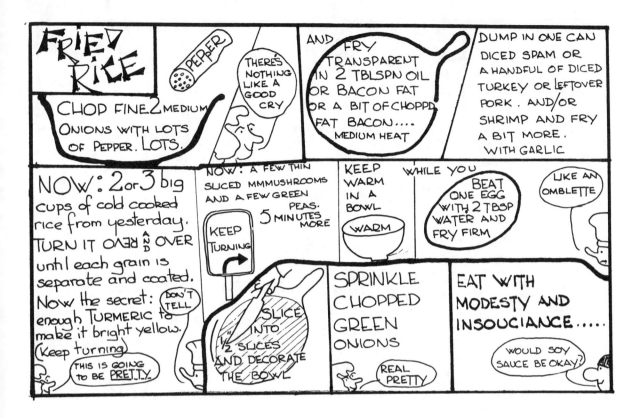

Fried Rice

This recipe is very close to a Javanese dish called Nasi Goreng, and it is a meal unto itself, an extremely attractive dish of bright colours and exotic taste which is simple to make and can be as imaginative as your pocket will allow.

Always, when you cook rice, cook too much, and keep what you don't eat covered in the fridge. So the first thing you had better learn to do is cook rice properly. Have nothing to do with instant rice, it has neither taste nor substance. Brown rice has a tendency to get soggy in fried dishes, and I always use long grain white rice for this particular dish, mainly because it looks so pretty.

One cup of rice, two cups of water, and a pinch of salt. Put it in the heaviest pot you have, bring it quickly to the boil with the cover off, put the lid on tight and forget it for twenty minutes with the heat as low as you can get it. An asbestos pad under the pot helps keep the heat down. Don't touch it, don't stir it, don't worry or peek, just leave it while you do yesterday's dishes. It will be light and fluffy with the grains all separate.

Mushrooms, green peppers, celery all sliced thin, small pieces of broccoli, or leeks, almost any vegetable except potatoes are good as an addition to fried rice. Leftover pork, or beef, or chicken or turkey are all good in thin slivers, and canned lunch meat, or Chinese sausage—this is a cook's dish which just happens while you stand and talk.

The turmeric is a spice which you should be adventurous with. Keep turning the rice over as you add it. Don't stir, get your spoon or whatever underneath it, down at the bottom of the pan, and turn it over with a little care. And take it easy on the soy sauce until you have really tasted the turmeric.

Chop fine 2 medium onions with plenty of pepper and fry until transparent in 2 Tbsp oil or bacon fat. Add diced meat or shrimp and fry with some garlic. Add 2 or 3 c cold cooked rice and enough turmeric to turn it bright yellow. Add a few thinly sliced mushrooms and a few green peas. Cook 5 minutes more and keep dish warm. Combine 1 egg with 2 Tbsp water, add, and fry mixture until firm. Slice to serve. Eat with chopped green onions.

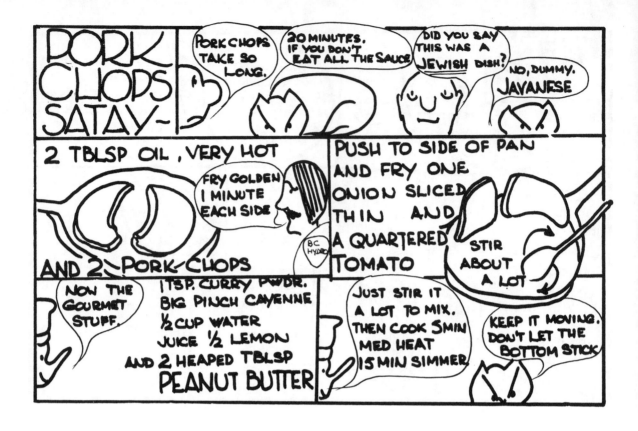

Pork Chops Satay

My mother, who is seventy-five, has just discovered the joys of illicit love, which she chooses to call "my friend." She blushes like a teenager every time he calls her "Dear," and she pretends in public not to look happy in case my father parts the clouds and sees her.

The joys that come late in life are not to be despised. It took me fifteen years of my life to discover women, twenty to get hooked on tobacco and another fifteen to get off it. I was thirty before mushrooms expanded the horizons of my consciousness, and forty before deciding that small cars were more fun than big ones.

But the most significant discovery of my life was peanut butter, courtesy of the United States Air Force, which seemed never to travel without it. When I tasted my first peanut butter sandwich I was twenty-two years old and since then have become an addict. Not peanut butter and jelly, certainly not with bananas, just plain old crunchy—preferably Deaf Smith (which comes from Texas)—untreated, unhomogenized peanut butter, the good kind which really sticks to your teeth, on toasted whole wheat bread, with just a sprinkle of

salt on it: the finest breakfast in the world.

If you were Javanese you would spend a long time grinding peanuts for dishes like this, unless you had a Cuisinart, roasted your own fresh nuts and ground them immediately into peanut butter. But all supermarket shelves have jars of the stuff. Once you start to use peanut butter there's no end to it.

And as my mother says, it's never too late to start.

Brown until golden 2 pork chops in 2 Tbsp very hot oil. Push chops to side of pan and fry 1 thinly sliced onion and 1 quartered tomato. Stir and add 1 tsp curry powder, 1 big pinch cayenne, ½ c water, juice of ½ lemon and 2 heaped Tbsp peanut butter. Stir and cook over medium heat for 5 minutes. Reduce heat and simmer 15 minutes, stirring frequently.

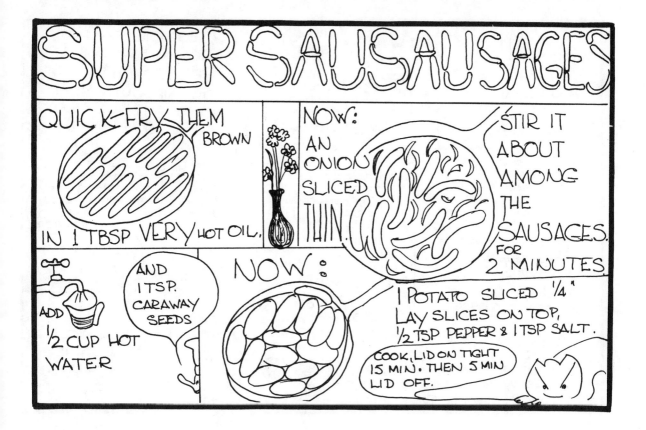

Super Sausages

Round the back of Victoria Station the hot chestnut men park their barrows at night. And the sandwich board men, those unfortunates who walk up and down with boards back and front advertising the least savoury of restaurants. (At least, they used to. Nowadays they tout the virtues of massage parlors and pornographic picture parlors.)

When I was young and given to drink, a habit which frequently resulted in missing the last train home, I frequently slept among the hot chestnut men. And ate 3:00 a.m. suppers with them. "Bangers," the British call sausages. Mostly they eat them with mashed potatoes. This is better.

Brown sausages in 1 Tbsp very hot oil. Add 1 onion, sliced thin, and stir with sausages for 2 minutes. Add ½ c hot water and 1 tsp caraway seeds. Add 1 potato, sliced ¼-inch thick, ½ tsp pepper and 1 tsp salt. Cook, covered tightly, 15 minutes. Then simmer 5 minutes with lid off.

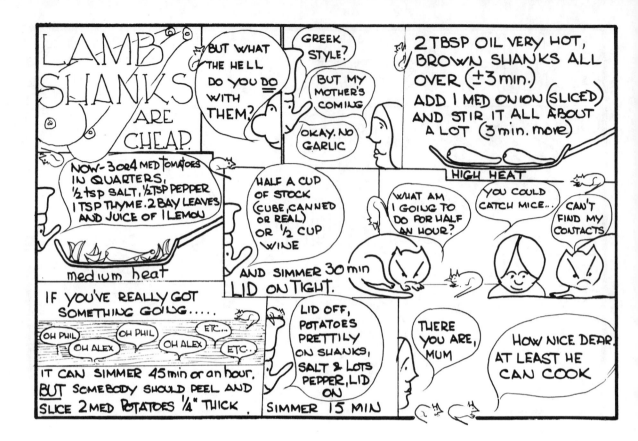

Lamb Shanks

Hot lamb roast on Sundays, cold on Mondays, minced on Tuesdays, and curried on Wednesdays—I was raised on lamb.

It seems, in retrospect, to have been nothing on Thursdays, fish of course on Friday, scrambled eggs on Saturday, and then it was Sunday all over again, and more lamb.

There was so much of it. Like the Christmas turkey, it went on forever. Lamb shanks are a way out. They are cheap, easy to figure out mathematically (one lamb shank, one person; two lamb shanks, two persons—you don't need a calculator) and they are infinitely variable. Lamb takes kindly to thyme, sage, oregano, parsley, curry powder, tomatoes, almost anything if you remember that if it doesn't taste exactly right what you have forgotten is the lemon.

Brown lamb shanks in 2 Tbsp very hot oil for about 3 minutes. Add 1 sliced medium onion and stir constantly for about 3 minutes. Add 3 or 4 quartered tomatoes, ½ tsp salt, ½ tsp pepper, 1 tsp thyme, 2 bay leaves and juice of 1 lemon. Add ½ c stock OR wine and simmer, covered, 30 minutes or longer. Slice 2 medium potatoes ¼-inch thick and lay on shanks. Add salt and plenty of pepper, cover and simmer 15 minutes.

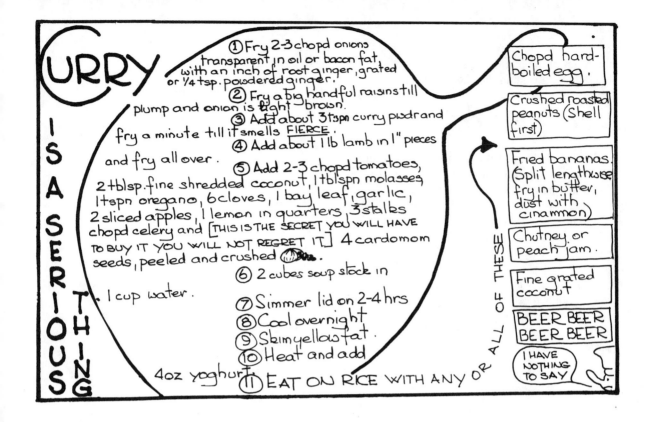

Curry

Cardamom seeds are little soft white fibrous shells which you open with your thumb nail and find inside half a dozen little hard black seeds. They must be crushed, either with a mortar and pestle, or set on a board and rolled with a beer bottle.

Beer is the only drink for a good curry, or, if you are feeling wealthy, gin and tonic. Tea is good too, but this curry is a party dish, a sharing dish, and is extremely economical. Six people can eat off one pound of meat, although there is nothing wrong with more if you feel like it.

I buy cheap imported lamb, which may look fat at the beginning, but don't worry. Two things will happen to the fat if you cook it gently and long enough. First of all, there will be chemical changes which firm it up and make it taste extremely sweet, and any excess will come to the top of the pot during the cooling overnight, and can be lifted off with a spoon.

Apart from cardamom seeds, the big secret in cooking curry is to fry the curry powder. It will go dark brown, and smell bright and fiercely bitter and clean out your sinuses and maybe make your eyes water. Very slow cooking is also essential. The man who showed me this recipe insisted that a curry was not a curry until you had slept with it, and in his restaurant there were indeed cooks curled up by their copper pots, large, two foot copper pots with small charcoal fires underneath.

I sometimes make a curry late at night, and let it simmer till breakfast. The meat may disintegrate, but it doesn't matter, the whole thing becomes a very rich, bitter-sweet, hot and delicious thick sauce to eat over rice. And it is infinitely extendable by the pretties you eat with it. Rice on a plate, curry on the rice, and goodies on the curry. None of this elegant dishing up, it is a nice, messy together dish, as complicated or as simple as you wish.

If you are going to fry bananas, don't get them too green. The ripest bananas are best. I usually buy the ones on special, that are just beginning to turn black. Peel them, cut them in half then lengthwise, so that each banana is four pieces. Fry them in butter both sides, till they are soft, lift

continued

them out of the pan to a dish, and dust them liberally with cinammon. Highly addictive.

Fry 2 or 3 chopped onions until transparent in oil or bacon fat with 1 inch of grated ginger root OR ¼ tsp powdered ginger. Fry a large handful of raisins until plump and onion is light brown. Add 3 tsp curry powder and fry 1 minute. Add 1 lb lamb cut in 1-inch pieces. Add 2 or 3 chopped tomatoes, 2 Tbsp finely shredded coconut, 1 Tbsp molasses, 1 tsp oregano, 6 cloves, 1 bay leaf, 1 clove garlic, 2 sliced apples, 1 quartered lemon, 3 stalks chopped celery and 4 peeled and crushed cardamom seeds. Add 2 soup stock cubes in 1 c water and simmer, covered, for 2 to 4 hours. To serve, see above.

Lamb and Anchovies

This sounds completely ridiculous. I know. But just try it. Don't worry if you don't like anchovies, by the time they are cooked they taste totally different. And don't fall back on the usual "I hate lamb." This method will resurrect just about any old piece of mutton, but if you are careful and get a really nice piece of fresh local lamb from the butcher it is a dish which you can make very easily, and delight whoever you happen to have for dinner. About three and a half pounds is the best size for four people. It will all get eaten, hot, and the flavour is completely delightful.

If you want to throw half a dozen medium-sized, peeled, whole onions into the pan an hour before it's cooked, that's nice. Then pour off the fat and make a little gravy. That's nice too. But nicest of all in lamb time is the zucchini time.

How to cook zucchini? Try this. Get nice, firm, good green zucchini. Slice them, unpeeled, into half-inch slices. Put a tablespoonful olive oil in your heaviest lidded saucepan, heat it medium 'til it's just short of smoking, and dump in the slices of zucchini with a clove of chopped garlic. Slosh them about a bit for three or four minutes until they start

to cook, and while that is happening squeeze the juice of half a lemon (or more next time) over everything. Turn the heat down to simmer, put the lid on and leave it all for ten or fifteen minutes. Oh yes, and a little salt, and some people like a little pepper. Serve it in a dish with all the juices.

And, if you want a quick dessert, just sprinkle a little instant coffee, a little cocoa powder on vanilla ice cream, and pour ordinary whiskey over it. Carefully. This cuts the working time for a complete dinner down to something like twenty minutes.

Smooth together 1 large mashed clove garlic and 1 small can anchovy fillets, including oil. Add 2 Tbsp brown sugar to form paste. Criss-cross fat on a lamb roast with a sharp knife and spread with anchovy paste. Heat 3 Tbsp oil in 400 degree oven until it sizzles. Add lamb and roast, basting after 5, 10 and 20 minutes. Turn oven down to 350 degrees and cook 30 minutes per pound.

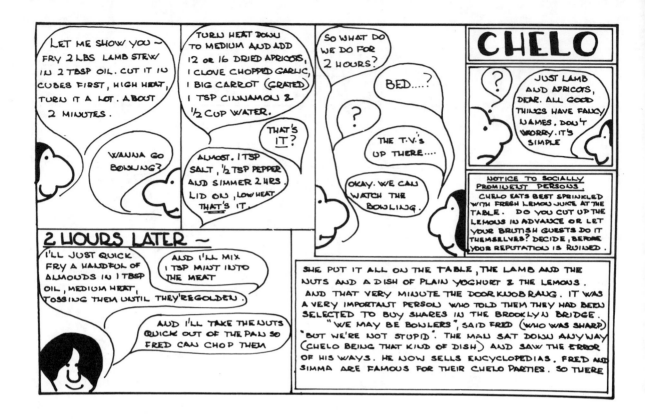

Chelo

Dried apricots are great for hiking snacks, lunch boxes, boat food and as candy for kids. I used to get bad looks from kids at Halloween when I offered them a handful of dried fruit instead of bubble gum, but as the years went by there appeared a hard core of kids who actually asked for fruit, which I thought was a triumph of common sense and proof of some nutritional instinct. Until I discovered that a local wheeler-dealer, aged ten, was trading in dried fruit, giving vast quantities of cheap candy for it, then selling it to his mother to make jam.

All over the world where fruit grows, people use dried fruit for cooking. In India, in Morocco, in Russia, in Persia—wherever people are poor, they dry such things as apricots because they don't have deep freezes, and then use them in the middle of winter to make a little meat go a long way.

Chelo is a poor people's dish. It keeps well (in fact, it's better next day), you can eat it with anything plain, like rice or pasta or pita bread, and you can fancy it up as much as your palate or level of society demands, with roasted almonds or with mint chopped into the yoghurt, and serve it with

good wine or mint tea. And if you are a midnight snacker, it is wonderful cold, just spooned out of the dish and reflected upon. Somehow it doesn't work well with beef, but if you want to use chicken instead of lamb you won't be disappointed.

Brown 2 lbs lamb, cubed, in 2 Tbsp oil over high heat, turning often. Reduce heat to medium and add 12 to 16 dried apricots, 1 clove chopped garlic, 1 large grated carrot, 1 tsp cinnamon and ½ c water. Then add 1 tsp salt, ½ tsp pepper and simmer, covered, 2 hours. Fry a handful of almonds in 1 Tbsp oil over medium heat, tossing until golden. Add 1 tsp mint to the meat. Chop nuts and serve as an accompaniment to the lamb, along with plain yoghurt and fresh squeezed lemon.

Lamb Chops Sofia

Sofia was tall and elegant and beautiful, and she thought that lamb chops were a last resort.

Lamb Chops Sofia evolved itself while she lighted the fire and washed my last week's dishes and swept the floor and made my bed and fed the cat and emptied the bath and generally behaved like a liberated woman. It is easy to make, with a nice long time to sit and decide that the day wasn't so bad after all. There is also only one pot to clean, and if you put in enough vegetables it is what the dieticians call a balanced meal.

I buy cheap lamb chops, shoulder chops. Any lamb at all can be made nice with a little love and care, and all lamb improves at least one hundred percent if you can possibly arrange to leave it marinating in the refrigerator overnight.

Marinades are a personal thing. Try about half and half oil and vinegar (or wine), a bit of fine chopped onion, a little salt, a little pepper, and (for lamb) some basil or rosemary or oregano. Lemon juice is nice too. Don't be scared of oregano, use lots. You don't need to make enough marinade to cover the meat, just mix a bit in a plate, dip both sides, and turn it occasionally. And if you have a cat put it somewhere inaccessible. I once had a cat which ate six marinating lamb chops in ten minutes while I took a shower.

Fry the chops quickly 'til they are brown, then turn down the heat. The rest is easy. Take a look occasionally, and if it is getting too dry, dump in a spoonful or two of water. Or wine. If you want to pretty it up, sprinkle a little chopped parsley before you serve, and put one lamb chop on each plate, on top of the rice.

Inexpensive and very filling.

Brown 2 lamb chops quickly over high heat. Add 1 tsp oregano, 1 chopped clove garlic, 1 chopped onion, 1 sliced green pepper (and/or 1 sliced leek), a few sliced mushrooms and two stalks sliced celery. Fry for 5 minutes, then add 2 sliced tomatoes, ½ sliced lemon, ⅓ c uncooked rice, ⅔ c water and 1 soup cube. Stir until it boils and simmer, covered, for 40 minutes.

Korma

Very bright, very colourful, and of course very easy. Most of the cooking happens while you're doing something else, so that life doesn't have to come to a grinding halt just because you've got people coming to supper.

Basically this is a Parsee dish, and the Parsees eat the best food in India, largely because they have absolutely no hang-ups and no religious prohibitions. If you're Jewish, they won't serve pork, if you're Hindu then there'll be no beef on the menu. Everything they cook is infinitely adaptable because food is first and foremost a social occasion.

Korma is a curry, but it's not intended to be a biker's special or an alternative to Drano. It will not make your hair fall out or smoke come out of your ears. It's mild and gentle and rich. And foolproof.

In a bowl mix 1 small carton yoghurt, 2 tsp turmeric and 1 clove of chopped garlic. Stir in 2 lbs pork shoulder, cubed, and let it marinate at least 2 hours. Slice 1 large onion thin and fry it in 2 tsp oil over medium heat. Add 6 cloves, 1 tsp pepper, 1 tsp salt and fry for 2 minutes. Add meat and yoghurt, rinse the bowl into the pan with ½ c water and simmer, covered, 45 minutes, stirring occasionally, until sauce thickens. Eat with rice, chickpeas or tortillas.

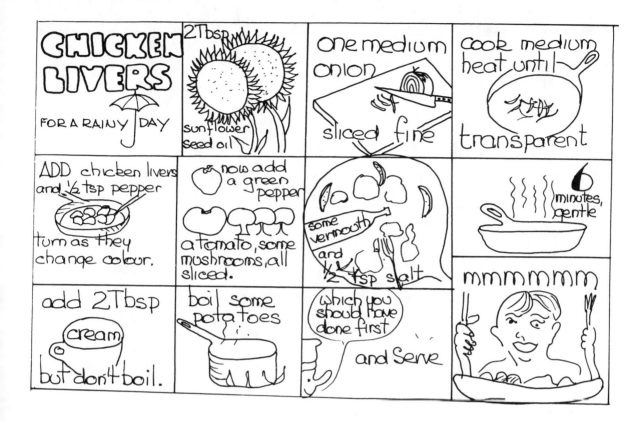

Rainy Day Chicken Livers

This is a rainy day dish that I always cook for two—and finish up eating with four.

It needs a bottle of wine—something pretty earthy such as Gamza, or Bardolino—and a loaf of fresh bread, real bread, the kind that doesn't come wrapped in plastic.

Also it is cheap, and quick.

Put the potatoes on to boil. Start them in cold water, with salt and mint.

Chop the onion. Cut up the other vegetables into something like one-inch pieces. Slice the mushrooms. Sit back for fifteen minutes.

I always start my cooking with the longest thing and count time from there. Potatoes take about half an hour, and the livers take about ten minutes. So, ten minutes before the potatoes are done, start the onions.

But, before you start, you have about fifteen minues to sit back and drink some of the vermouth. Or the sherry. Or the wine. I use vermouth because I like it, but friends use brandy or sherry. Anything with a wine flavour will do.

The important word is gentle. Turn things over. Don't keep dabbing at them with the fork. Just turn them over.

I use chopsticks for a lot of things, it makes for good habits. The Chinese stores sell cooking chopsticks that are joined together at the top by a small string and can hang by the stove.

Use lots of basil. If it comes out of a supermarket jar, crush it before you use it. If you haven't got a mortar and pestle, then use two spoons or, nicer still, put it in the palm of your hand and rub it around with your thumb until it smells nice. And use lots. About twice as much as you think you should. About a spoonful before you crush it. And another pinch for luck. And about half a teaspoonful of salt.

Use these things, until they feel right. If you have to cook with measuring spoons and a balance, you might just as well become a druggist, which you won't like.

Coat everything with oil, gently. And, when the vegetables begin to change colour and look shiny, add the vermouth or the sherry.

Cook for about six minutes, then add the cream. Bring the heat back up, but don't boil it. Serve it

continued

on rice, or potatoes, with peas. Mop up the sauce that's left with bread, finish the wine, sit back and burp.

Boil new potatoes, starting them in cold water with salt and mint. Chop onion and cut other vegetables into 1-inch pieces. Slice mushrooms. Twenty minutes after potatoes are started, cook onions with pepper in sunflower oil until transparent. Add chicken livers and turn gently as they change color. Add green pepper, tomatoes, ½ tsp salt, plenty of basil and vermouth. Cook gently for 6 minutes. Add ¼ to ½ c cream to pan, but do not boil. Serve with new potatoes.

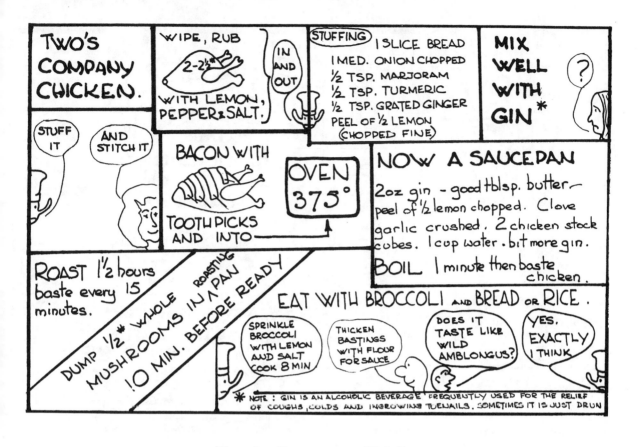

Two's Company Chicken

Gin?

If this recipe used juniper berries, nobody would make it. Because juniper berries are hard to find. The distillers buy a lot of them to make gin.

Gin is not fashionable in kitchens. But, if you learn to cook with it, you will always keep some on hand. It's good for rubbing backs, or cleaning false teeth, for thinning paint or anesthetizing flies. In cooking, it does a lot for almost any drab meat.

Something happens in the cooking and, instead of tame domesticated bland chicken flavour, there comes a most aromatic smell, and the taste of wild game, like partridges that have been feeding all summer on berries.

When you make the stuffing, just put in enough to make it stick together. And, the better the bread, the better the stuffing. Rye bread, or sourdough, or good crusty French bread, or even cooked rice.

It's all simple, which is just as well because most beginners with a bottle of gin tend to become a little confused after the second basting.

Try to get root ginger if you can. The flavour is much better than powdered. Most supermarkets sell it and it will keep in the fridge wrapped in a piece of foil until you want to cook some Chinese food.

Wipe chicken and rub inside and out with lemon, salt and pepper. Mix a stuffing of 1 slice bread, 1 medium chopped onion, ½ tsp marjoram, ½ tsp turmeric, ½ tsp grated ginger, peel of ½ lemon chopped fine, all mixed with gin to moisten. Stuff bird and cover with slices of bacon. Roast in 375 degree oven for 1½ hours, basting with sauce (follows) every 15 minutes. For sauce combine 2 oz gin, 1 Tbsp butter, chopped peel of ½ lemon, 1 clove garlic, 2 chicken stock cubes, 1 c water and a small amount gin. Boil 1 minute. Add ½ lb whole mushrooms 10 minutes before serving.

Chicken and Rye

This happened one cold and windy night on Keats Island. We were well snugged up with the oil lamp going, a cribbage board and a bottle of Jack Daniels, rather hoping that the wind would get worse and nobody else would arrive, when about sixty feet of wall to wall fibreglass tied up across the float, complete, we later saw, with air conditioning, washer and dryer, television and a microwave oven.

Their generator had packed up. Could we heat them some water for instant coffee? We asked them for supper, and they arrived, most apologetically, with a bottle of Crown Royal, which, not to offend (and even more, not to deplete the Jack Daniels, which we figured to last a couple of days) we used to cook supper. They were delighted, and since then it has been a favourite, because most boats, like most well ordered houses, have a little rye around. It's even better with Jack Daniels. But so's just about everything.

Fry 2 chopped garlic cloves for 1 minute in 3 Tbsp hot oil. Add chicken pieces and brown lightly. Add 2 oz rye, sprinkle with a lot of tarragon and cook, covered, for 15 minutes. Remove cover and cook 1 minute. Serve with rice.

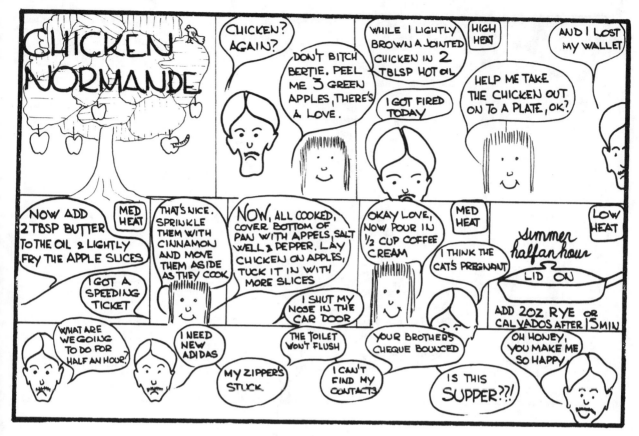

Chicken Normande

Calvados, the white lightning of Normandy, is a wonderful drink sometimes known in the U.S. as applejack. When I was riding a motorbike in one of our attempts to defend democracy the French would fill my waterbottle with Calvados (I could never figure out if this meant they were for me or agin me), frequent slugs of which made the pursuit of freedom and the life of a humble corporal considerably more bearable.

In the evening we would cook. We spent considerable time on a beach to which the U.S. Army had delivered vast quantities of canned chicken. Neighbouring beaches had equally vast quantities of canned peaches, and one beach was rumoured to have dried onions sufficient to supply the entire Allied Armies for six months. We ate canned chicken raw, cold, hot, lukewarm and with our fingers, and hated it. We drank the Calvados, which made us hate it a little less, but finally we discovered the value of combining the two.

Since that time I have refused (on deeply religious grounds) to have anything to do with canned chicken. But Calvados I'll drink any time. If you can't find Calvados, use rye, or bourbon; the apples and cream will make it almost as good, particularly if you have a couple of belts while it's cooking.

Lightly brown a cut-up chicken in 2 Tbsp hot oil over high heat. Meanwhile peel 3 green apples. Remove chicken from the pan and add 2 Tbsp butter to the oil. Lighly brown apple slices over medium heat. Cover bottom of pan with apples, salt and pepper well, lay chicken on apples and tuck more slices around chicken. Pour in ½ c cream and simmer, covered, ½ hour over low heat, adding 2 oz Rye OR Calvados after first 15 minutes.

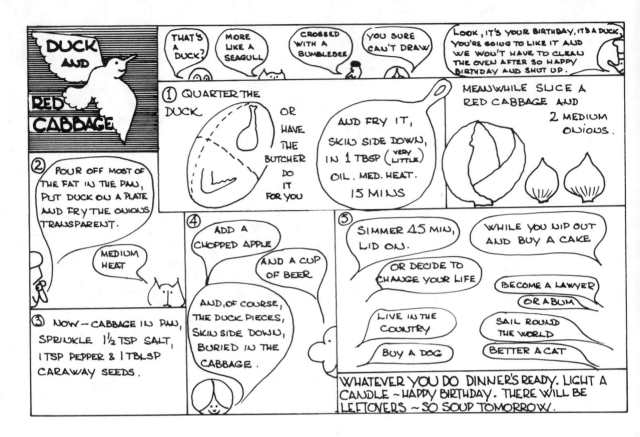

Duck and Red Cabbage

I'm not entirely sure that the leftover soup isn't the best part of any dinner, particularly if the party people (in this case two of you) are still around. (It does happen that way. I have friends who met at a New Year's Eve bash, walked home with one another and never walked out again; they're still enjoying variations on the theme of their original party.)

Even if it doesn't turn out to be some enchanted evening, enjoy the duck and then clear the table. Shove all the leftovers, except cake or other sweet stuff, into your biggest saucepan: potatoes or noodles, rice, salad, bones, uneaten duck (or turkey, or chicken), vegetables, just *everything*. Bring to a boil, put the lid on and simmer, just forget about it—on the lowest heat, for two or three hours, even, if you're comfortable with simmering, overnight.

Let cool with the lid slightly ajar, skim off all the visible fat, pick out the biggest pieces of meat, and strain the rest. The juice may need a little salt, but what I do is add a lot of pepper and a tablespoon of vinegar for an instant hot and sour soup. Or you can put a big teaspoon of thyme in it, and some

vegetables cut very thin and you've got an instant potage. Whatever you do to it, leftover soup can't go wrong; it has that legendary back-of-the-stove, French farmhouse quality that people rave about.

Quarter a duck and fry it, skin side down in 1 Tbsp oil over medium heat. Meanwhile slice a red cabbage and 2 medium onions. Pour most of the fat out of the pan, move duck to a plate and fry onions over medium heat until transparent. Add cabbage and sprinkle with 1½ tsp salt, 1 tsp pepper and 1 Tbsp caraway seeds. Add 1 chopped apple and 1 c beer, the duck pieces (skin side down) and the cabbage. Simmer 45 minutes.

CHICKEN
AND
WATERMELON

CHICKEN
AND
WATERMELON

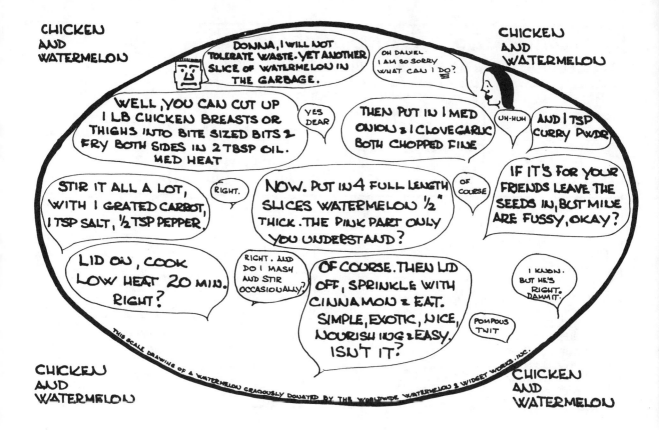

CHICKEN
AND
WATERMELON

CHICKEN
AND
WATERMELON

Chicken and Watermelon

There comes a time when sitting on the porch spitting watermelon seeds interferes with serious conversation. Besides, the seeds pile up after a while, the mailman slips on them and muggers use them for ammunition. But what to do? Every year watermelons get bigger and cheaper; every year the season gets longer.

Four of us, faced with an 18-pound monster, decided to take our solutions past the making of watermelon ice cream, beyond watermelon frappé and simple watermelon juice (all of them excellent but still undeniably watermelon). Fried watermelon just doesn't work very well, and the zucchini loaf freaks, carrot cake fiends and potato bread purists all draw the line at incorporating watermelon into their recipes.

Finally, as frequently happens after the second bottle of wine is opened, the obvious became obvious. Since chicken and watermelon usually come home in the same shopping bag, why not examine their potential for co-existence.

Chicken and watermelon has a fragile, evasive, delicate taste. It's easy to prepare, very pleasant on the palate, and uniquely North American.

A little rice with it is nice, maybe a couple of fried bananas dusted with cinnamon, or a handful of chopped roasted peanuts. But no matter how you serve it, you have every reason to look smug.

Fry 1 lb of bite sized pieces of chicken breasts or thighs in 2 Tbsp oil over medium heat. Add 1 medium onion and 1 clove garlic, both chopped fine, and 1 tsp curry powder. Add 1 grated carrot, 1 tsp salt and ½ tsp pepper. Add 4 ½-inch strips of seeded and peeled watermelon and simmer for 20 minutes, mashing and stirring occasionally. Sprinkle with cinnamon and serve hot.

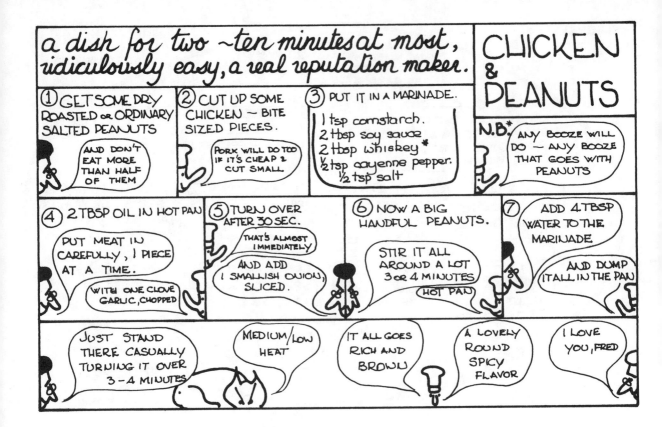

Chicken and Peanuts

The most difficult part of making this dish is preventing your guests from eating the ingredients. So hide the peanuts until you're ready to cook, then do it quicker than a three-card monte hustler. After you have made this dish with chicken breasts, move on to the cheaper parts like thighs and legs (by this time you'll think nothing of cutting the bones out), and finally start to buy whole chickens and make soup and stock with the back and wings.

How to make stock? A big pot, all the bits of chicken you don't use, an onion cut up and a carrot. Cover with water, bring to a boil, skim the froth off after 15 minutes (it's easy with a spoon—you don't *have* to have a skimmer), turn the heat down as low as it will go and let it simmer, lid on, all night, or at least while you go to a movie. Strain the stock into a jar, keep it in the fridge and use it to cook with; or add a few chopped vegetables and a little salt and pepper for instant soup.

Make this dish first with peanuts. Then try almonds, or cashews, even walnuts. Coconuts are not recommended unless you're cooking an ostrich.

Cut chicken OR pork into bite sized pieces. Marinate meat in 1 tsp cornstarch, 2 Tbsp soy sauce, 2 Tbsp whiskey, ½ tsp cayenne pepper and ½ tsp salt. Put meat pieces, one at a time, into 2 Tbsp hot oil, reserving marinade. Add 1 clove chopped garlic. Turn meat in 30 seconds and add 1 small sliced onion. Add a large handful of dry roasted or salted peanuts and stir, cooking for 3 or 4 minutes. Add 4 Tbsp water to reserved marinade and add marinade to the pan, stirring every 3 or 4 minutes over medium-low heat.

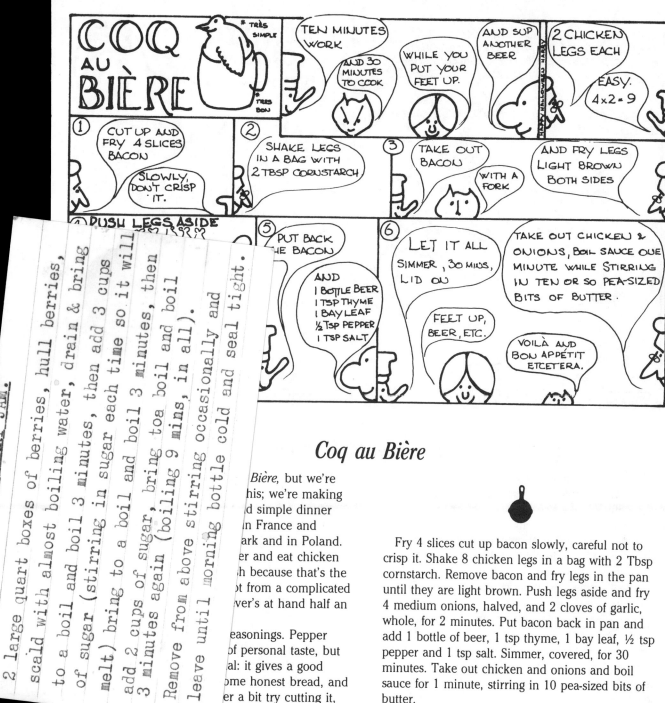

Coq au Bière

Bière, but we're
his; we're making
d simple dinner
n France and
ark and in Poland.
er and eat chicken
h because that's the
t from a complicated
ver's at hand half an

easonings. Pepper
of personal taste, but
al: it gives a good
me honest bread, and
er a bit try cutting it,
half and half, ...er, which the British
call a shandy. The easiest way to find ginger beer
is to follow a Jamaican: they drink it at home and
have an underground network for finding it
elsewhere.

Fry 4 slices cut up bacon slowly, careful not to
crisp it. Shake 8 chicken legs in a bag with 2 Tbsp
cornstarch. Remove bacon and fry legs in the pan
until they are light brown. Push legs aside and fry
4 medium onions, halved, and 2 cloves of garlic,
whole, for 2 minutes. Put bacon back in pan and
add 1 bottle of beer, 1 tsp thyme, 1 bay leaf, ½ tsp
pepper and 1 tsp salt. Simmer, covered, for 30
minutes. Take out chicken and onions and boil
sauce for 1 minute, stirring in 10 pea-sized bits of
butter.

Eight-Legged Chicken

You have to prepare this early, before the guests arrive. Don't drink too much while you're doing it or it will look like a low budget horror movie; and try to get someone to help you, because a secret shared is containable. People think you're crazy if you walk around alone for an hour before dinner smiling that secret smirk, but if there are two of you smiling they just think you're overreacting to sex in the afternoon.

I don't overstuff chickens because they take so much longer to cook. I just poke a few bits of something nice inside their back door—some chopped lemons and a handful of garlic, or some chopped onions and a teaspoonful of thyme. Or some chopped apples. Or just lemon juice and tarragon. I rub them well with salt (makes the skin crisp), I use a 400-degree oven, and I baste them every 15 minutes with butter. This chicken goes brown all over, and if you don't have too many lights on (candles are best) people can't see the stitches. When they stop laughing you just snip the thread and suddenly everybody's got supper. It doesn't work with a turkey, but it will with a capon, and there it is, an unforgettable dinner for ten.

When you get really skillful at the stitching, next thing you know you'll be doing nose jobs for your friends.

Buy a chicken and 6 extra legs. Stitch extra legs onto the chicken using cotton thread. Stuff the chicken with some chopped lemons and a handful of garlic OR some chopped onions and 1 tsp thyme OR just lemon juice and tarragon. Rub chicken well with salt and baste chicken every 15 minutes while it cooks in a 400-degree oven.

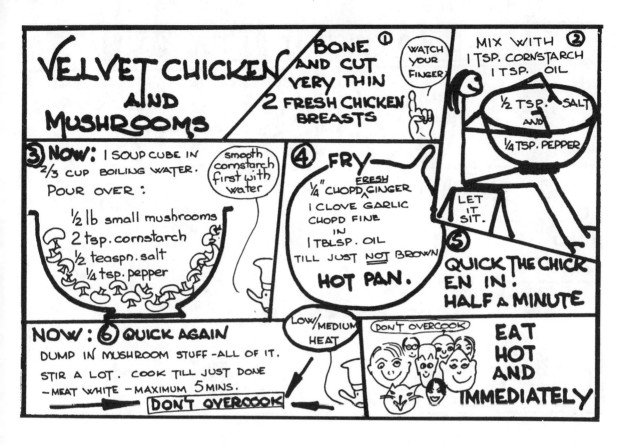

Velvet Chicken and Mushrooms

Fresh ginger you can buy in almost any enlightened supermarket, strange, lumpy-looking tan-coloured roots, from Hawaii. And they are something you should learn to use.

Most simple Chinese vegetable dishes are flavoured with fresh root ginger, just a bit, shredded into bean sprouts. And most very bad Chinese restaurant food is made with shredded cooked chicken. If you learn to use fresh chicken, cut to size before it is cooked, and cooked very little, you will quickly come to an appreciation of what Chinese food really tastes like.

It's really quite easy. All you need is a sharp knife. Slide it close to the bones, and get off as much meat as you can in one piece. What is left on the bones will, with an onion, and simmered gently while you eat dinner, make a magnificent light soup for tommorrow's dinner, particularly if you remember to bring home a few mushrooms to slice into it, and even more particularly if you shred just a little ginger into it while it simmers.

This particular recipe is called Maw Gwooh Chow Ghuy Pien if you want to be smart. It is very simple, very smooth, and very spicy, a quick and easy thing to make in fifteen minutes. Just don't overcook it. Don't overcook it. Don't overcook it.

The chicken will turn a nice delicate white. If you want to make it even more exotic (although this is, I think, an unnecessary sophistication), replace a glass of the stock with a glass of sherry. But whatever you do, don't overcook it.

Bone and cut very thin 2 chicken breasts. Mix chicken with 1 tsp cornstarch, 1 tsp salt and ¼ tsp pepper. Let sit. Dissolve 1 soup cube in ⅔ c boiling water and pour over ½ lb small mushrooms, 2 tsp cornstarch, ½ tsp salt and ¼ tsp pepper. Fry ¼-inch piece chopped fresh ginger and 1 finely chopped clove garlic in 1 Tbsp oil, but do not brown. Quick fry chicken for 30 seconds in oil, then add mushroom mixture, stirring constantly until just done, no more than 5 minutes, over medium-low heat. Serve immediately.

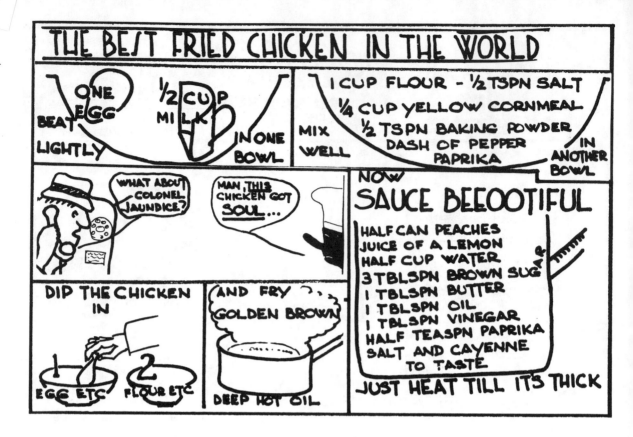

The Best Fried Chicken in the World

One not too distant day it will appear on the television screens and the supermarket shelves, in the papers and the magazines, anywhere that a million dollars can buy advertising. And a million can-opening cooks will buy it and, like all can-opening cooks, be disappointed without knowing why.

"SOUL" it will be called, "just add a pinch to everything." There will be a picture of a smiling lady, and some smiling children, and perhaps a smiling man. Probably with Colonel Whatsit beaming from a background of smiling black faces.

This recipe came to me from a smiling black face in the middle of New York. But she was careful to point out that soul isn't the monopoly of any colour or race and it doesn't come out of a bottle or packet. "It's sharing what there is with who there is." Princess Pamela has since written a cookbook but, long before that, when I was cold and had no money, she fed me fried chicken, gave me wine, and told me the recipe.

She had a little restaurant that seated sixteen. And she cooked in a kitchen the size of a broom closet, without fancy pots or thermostats—not even

a fan. She measured things with the palm of her hand—a little palmful was a teaspoon, a big one a tablespoon. She fried in a big old pan with two or three inches of oil in it, and she always had the plates hot. And when she felt like it, she would sit down and talk to the customers.

You can cook this fried chicken on a two-burner hotplate with one saucepan—make the sauce first, then wipe it out and make the chicken. Strain the oil when it's cold through an old nylon stocking, and put it in a jar ready for the next time around.

In a bowl beat 1 egg and ½ c milk. In another bowl combine 1 c flour, ½ tsp salt, ¼ c yellow cornmeal, ½ tsp baking powder and a dash of pepper and paprika. Dip chicken first in egg, then in flour mixture, then deep fry until golden. Meanwhile make a sauce of ½ can peaches, juice of 1 lemon, ½ c water, 3 Tbsp brown sugar, 1 Tbsp butter, 1 Tbsp vinegar, ½ tsp paprika, and salt and cayenne pepper to taste. Heat sauce until thick and serve with chicken.

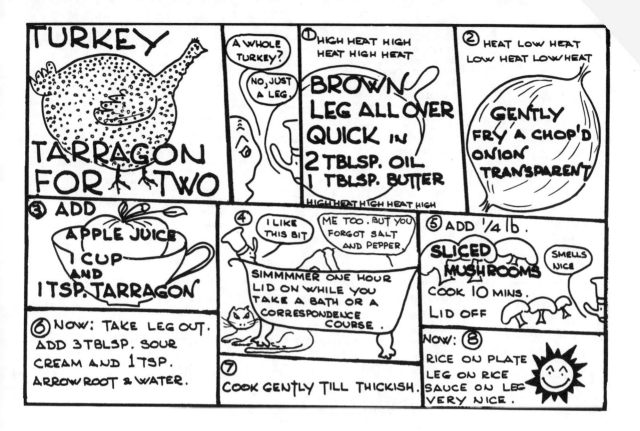

Turkey Tarragon for Two

This is a very simple version of a well known classic, *Poulet à L'Estragon*. It was taught to me by a girl in Normandy, who also taught me to steal chickens.

The chickens of Normandy were big and tough and old. And the stolen ones were cheap. Turkey legs are a substitute which fills most of these requirements, but if you do happen to have a butcher who keeps his chickens Normandy-farmer-style he will probably expect you to steal them.

So here's how you do it. The chickens sleep in apple trees, on branches about four feet off the ground. They must be snuck up upon, very quietly, from behind, with one hand from above, and one from below. You very carefully and slowly bring the two hands together at exactly the same moment, keeping firm hold with the lower one while the upper one helps the chicken off the branch quietly and quickly under your jacket. You then run.

My instructor was a purist. She felt that chicken stealing was a natural predatory act, in tune with nature. In order to get properly in tune, etc., she insisted that we spend the evening waiting for the right moment (usually two or three in the morning) getting our natural rhythms ready.

So if you have a butcher whose chickens sleep in trees in an apple orchard which has a haystack close by, all you need is a partner interested in natural rhythms and you will have a really authentic Normandy chicken....

If you haven't got arrowroot, use two teaspoons cornstarch. But arrowroot is much better; it's smoother, and translucent.

Brown 1 turkey leg over high heat in 2 Tbsp oil and 1 Tbsp butter. Turn heat to low and gently fry 1 chopped onion until transparent. Add 1 c apple juice and 1 tsp tarragon. Salt and pepper to taste. Simmer, covered, for 1 hour. Add ¼ lb sliced mushrooms and cook 10 minutes, uncovered. Take leg out and add 3 Tbsp sour cream and 1 tsp arrowroot or cornstarch dissolved in 1 tsp water. Cook gently until thickened.

Chicken and Dumplings

There comes a time, usually in the winter, when the cat is lost, your lover has gone, the car won't start and the buses are on strike, the cheque didn't come, the lab tests were positive ("but not to worry," said the doctor, "come in on Monday"), the plumbing is blocked and the landlord won't fix it, and life looks and sounds like an afternoon soap on black-and-white TV. This is when we need the classic *Saturday Evening Post* grandmother. We need freckles on our faces and a long drive out to the farm and most of all—sharp, sophisticated and city-slick as we may be—we need a cuddle.

You can go out and buy Mother Somebody's Homestyle Dinner, but it won't taste half as good as this, you won't get any pleasure out of making it, and nobody gives rave reviews to a packet. Just remember, always check the baking powder. Drop half a teaspoon in a little water. If it doesn't fizz, get some fresh.

There's nothing nicer than hearing your stomach say: "There, there, dear, everything's going to be fine." So dry your eyes, drink your milk, and don't eat all those cookies; you'll spoil your dinner...

Fry 10 to 12 chicken thighs in 2 Tbsp oil. Meanwhile slice 2 large carrots and chop coarse 2 medium onions and 1 clove garlic. When chicken is light brown, toss vegetables with chicken and oil. Add 1 tsp pepper, 1 tsp green dill, 1 tsp salt and 1 can of corn. Add 1½ c hot water and simmer, covered, for 30 minutes.

Mix 1 c flour, ½ tsp salt, 2 tsp baking powder, 1 egg and ½ c milk just until moist. Add a large handful of chopped parsley. Spoon tablespoonfuls of batter into cooked chicken dish, cover, and simmer 10 minutes.

Chicken and Oranges

Honest, simple, colourful, light, nourishing, different, easy, quick.

There was a time when I chose to believe that first-class passengers on airplanes actually had a little kitchen up front, with a French chef, a row of copper pots, and tanks full of live lobsters. Then one day I flew first class. We got free booze and food that was different from the proletariats' back there in tourist, or coach, or whatever they were calling the uncomfortable seats that year. But it wasn't any better.

This is a refinement of that day's *Poulet à l'Orange*. It's simpler and much better. If you want to fancy it up, add a little sherry with the orange juice, or grate a little fresh ginger into the pan at the start. Silver plates, paper ones or fingers, this is a very nice dish indeed. Use breasts the first time you try a new chicken dish; switch to thighs, which are cheaper but taste better. But remember, you'll need your sharpest knife to bone them.

Chop 2 chicken breasts or 4 thighs into bite sized pieces and toss them in a bag with 2 Tbsp cornstarch. Fry them over medium heat in 2 Tbsp butter for 3 minutes. Meanwhile peel an orange and put segments into the pan, tossing with butter. Stir in 1 small onion or a bunch of green onions chopped fine, ½ tsp salt and ½ tsp pepper. Cover and cook 7 minutes on medium-low heat. Remove mixture from pan and add ½ c orange juice and a small amount of chopped parsley, scraping the bottom of the pan. Boil 1 minute, then pour over chicken and serve hot.

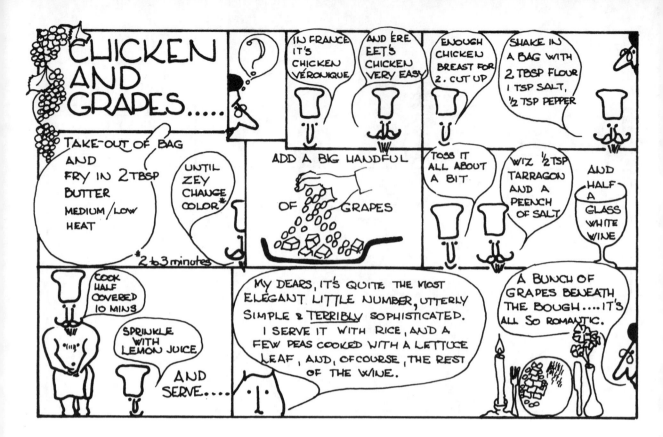

Chicken and Grapes

There's something elegant about grapes: they're not anything you associate with beer and potato chips. And there's something virtuous about them as you can tell when you take grapes to people in hospital and they're too sick to eat them so you sit and console and one by one they disappear into your mouth. You feel so *good.*

Try sprinkling the inside of a chicken with pepper and salt, then a big teaspoonful of tarragon and the juice of half a lemon. Then poke a bunch of grapes in there. Nothing fussy, just poke them in and cook the chicken in a hot oven (400 degrees). Baste it occasionally with a little butter and in an hour you've got something wonderful.

A few grapes for dessert—pull them off the stalks and let them sit in a glass of white wine while you eat the chicken. Or put them unadorned on the table with a bowl of ice water alongside, some slices of lemon sitting in it. Washing the grapes at table is one way to get religion without being born again.

To get back to the original recipe—what else do you know that's both elegant and totally foolproof, and takes 15 minutes' preparation at the most?

Cut up enough chicken for two and shake it in a bag with 2 Tbsp flour, 1 tsp salt and ½ tsp pepper. Fry in 2 Tbsp butter on medium-low heat 2 to 3 minutes. Add a big handful of grapes and toss with ½ tsp tarragon and a pinch of salt. Add a glass of white wine and cook, covered, for 10 minutes. Sprinkle with lemon juice and serve with rice.

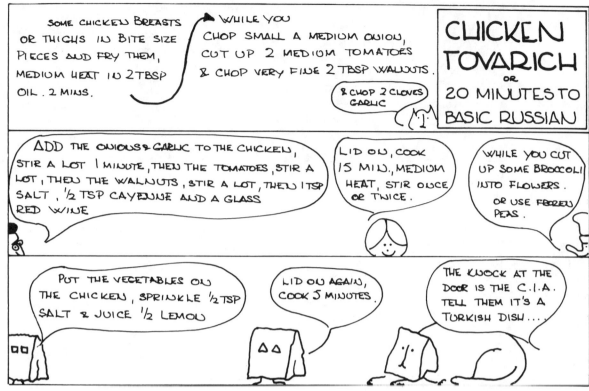

DO NOT ADMIT TO STRANGERS THAT YOU COOK RUSSIAN FOOD.

Chicken Tovarich

Wolves, beautiful women in horse-drawn sleighs, ice and snow everywhere, and potatoes and vodka. You know what Russia is like. A primitive version of North Dakota.

It was quite a shock to find that there are light, joyous, sunny dishes in Russia, food made with sun-warmed fruits, and as exciting as any Italian ever imagined—all of them easy to make and most of them digestible, even without vodka.

I was shown this dish using pomegranate juice, which is hard to get. Red wine is a perfectly acceptable substitute; or you can use cranberry juice with an extra clove of garlic and a teaspoonful of vinegar, or plain grape juice with a little vinegar and some orange peel. Don't get bogged down in dogma; just enjoy this thick, dark red, flavourful dish. If you have sauce left over, keep it in a cup in the fridge and use it on spaghetti.

Cut chicken breasts or thighs into bite sized pieces and fry them over medium heat in 2 Tbsp oil for 2 minutes. Meanwhile chop a medium onion, cut up 2 medium tomatoes, and chop very fine 2 Tbsp walnuts and 2 cloves garlic. Add onions and garlic to the chicken, stirring constantly for 1 minute, then add tomatoes, walnuts, 1 tsp salt, ½ tsp cayenne and 1 glass red wine, stirring between each addition. Cover and cook 15 minutes over medium heat, stirring once or twice. Cut up broccoli into flowers (or use frozen peas). Put the vegetables on the chicken, sprinkle with ½ tsp salt and the juice of ½ lemon. Cover and cook 5 minutes.

Chicken Wings Are Cheap

Dogs when very hungry will lick the fingers of people who have eaten fried chicken, but people, despite what the commercials say, are usually more interested in finding a paper towel to get the stuff off before they have to take their pants to the cleaners.

Real finger lickin' chicken is indeed rare, and it's not that popular. This recipe is certainly not for WASP cocktail parties, or indeed any party where white gloves are required. This chicken is sticky, messy and wonderful, and I like to go at it sitting around a table with a couple of good friends and a little Jack Daniels Black. But if you want to make these wings for a party, get everything ready beforehand and be prepared to stand at the stove making batches as fast as people eat them.

That's how you establish a reputation.

Cut chicken wings in 3 pieces (see above). Place chicken pieces in a pan and cover with ¼ inch water. Add 4 Tbsp soy sauce, 4 Tbsp vinegar, 1 tsp cayenne, 1 tsp hot mustard and 2 Tbsp sugar. Boil vigorously. When water is reduced by half, add 2 Tbsp oil. Turn wings frequently and reduce heat to medium. Chicken will turn dark brown and sauce will become sticky. Sprinkle cooked chicken wings with sesame seeds.

Chicken Livers and Grapes

In France they use duck livers and some very fancy booze called Armagnac. We don't have much of either, so I reworked this recipe into standard supermarket ingredients. Which of course is the only way to cook. Use what's handy, and do your best.

This is a ridiculously simple dish which can stand up against anybody's pretensions of haute cuisine. It is quite wonderful when cherries are used instead of grapes, and if you want to be really imaginative you can whizz it through the blender, put it in little bowls, chill it for an hour or so and serve it as a mousse. All good things are simpler than we think.

Lay 1 lb chicken livers over bottom of a pan. Sprinkle with ½ tsp salt and ½ tsp pepper. Cover tightly and cook over very low heat for 20 minutes. Warm a large handful of seedless grapes with a small amount of water in another pan over low heat. Drain the liquid off the livers and keep for soup. Splash 2 Tbsp rye or bourbon over livers. Combine grapes with livers and warm together over low heat for 1 minute. Serve with rice or on toast.

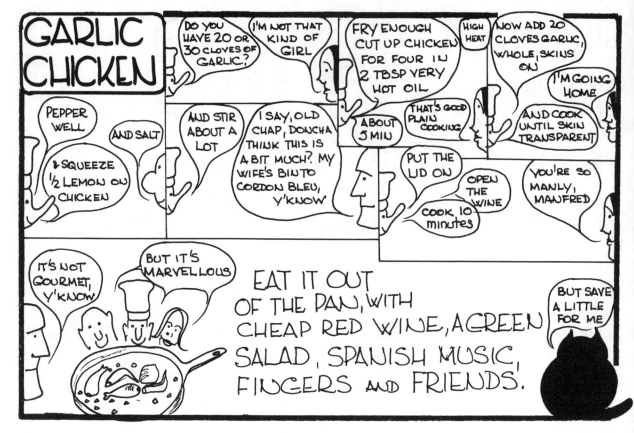

Garlic Chicken

Just don't tell 'em. Not unless you can trust 'em. You pick up a clove, put it close and squeeze the skin. The middle pops out into your mouth. It tastes as soft and gentle as lichee nuts, not at all like garlic. Once they get the feel of it they'll want more.

And garlic cooked in its skin is totally different from minced or chopped or pressed garlic. I frequently do it in stews—throw in two or three unpeeled cloves. They are easy to find and remove when you serve, especially when you have to lie a bit and tell them "No" when asked if there's garlic in it.

If you do think you smell a bit, the best thing is to start on your fingers, which you wash under a running cold tap. Hot water makes the oil go into your skin, cold rinses it away. On your breath a handful of parsley chewed well, or a belt of the freshest orange juice you can find. If there are two of you it shouldn't matter (because this is not the kind of dish you make for total strangers) and if there's a whole gang of you, then you can have a nice time discovering just how different it is from one person to another.

Don't be scared of garlic. There's nothing wrong with my social life.

Fry enough cut up chicken for four in 2 Tbsp very hot oil, about 5 minutes. Add 20 cloves whole unskinned garlics and cook until transparent. Pepper and salt well and squeeze ½ lemon on chicken. Cover and cook 10 minutes.

Chicken and Scotch

I really stole this recipe from the Four Seasons. We had just finished a twelve-hour stint in the studio, the lights had fried our brains, and what we needed was a rest. So we rented a suite with a big bath and a television set, a view of the mountains and room service.

After a bath, the champagne and some strawberries, we decided that room service was decadent, and went down to the dining room. And there it was, Chicken Breasts with Scotch, raising eyebrows among all the certified gourmets. It is simple and wonderful. If you don't like Scotch it tastes equally good with bourbon.

Squeeze ½ lime OR lemon over each deboned chicken breast and let marinate for an hour or longer. Flatten thin deboned breasts between waxed paper. Flour each breast on both sides and fry in hot butter over medium-high heat for 1 minute on each side. Pour in 1 oz scotch and flame over high heat, shaking as it flames. Serve immediately with rice.

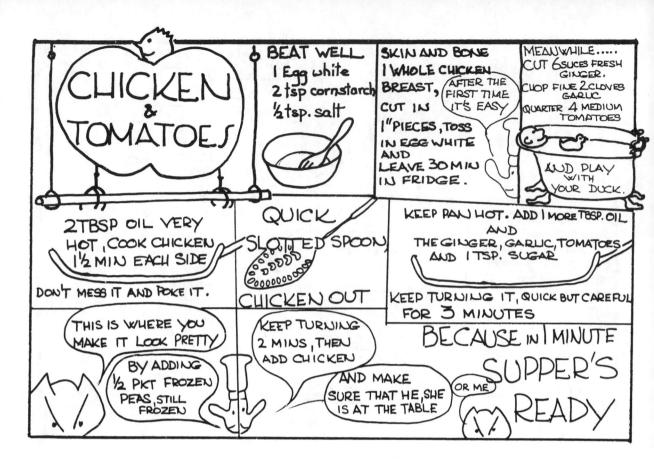

Chicken and Tomatoes

This is the quickest and simplest dish I know. Colourful and bright, it never goes wrong, a Chinese dish which you can't get better even in a Chinese restaurant because the moment of truth comes from eating it the moment it's cooked.

Just get everybody ready, let them wait for you to get out of the bath, make your entrance, be calm, change the record, water a couple of plants, hum a bit, and if you have the kind of mate who asks, "What the hell do you think you're doing?" just say you're in an insouciant mood.

Combine and beat well 1 egg white, 2 tsp cornstarch and ½ tsp salt. Skin and bone 1 whole chicken breast and cut in 1-inch pieces. Toss chicken with egg mixture and leave 30 minutes in refrigerator. Meanwhile cut 6 slices fresh ginger, chop fine 2 cloves garlic and quarter 4 medium tomatoes. Cook chicken in 2 Tbsp very hot oil 1½ minutes on each side. Take chicken out quickly, and keeping pan hot, add 1 Tbsp oil and the ginger, garlic, tomatoes and 1 tsp sugar. Keep turning chicken quickly for 3 minutes. Add ½ packet frozen peas, turn for another 2 minutes and return chicken to pan.

African Chicken

I was trying to copy a dish dimly remembered from a Malaysian restaurant. And she was a newspaper lady with a smile, a hat and white gloves, a real ladies' pages newspaper lady looking for scoops on engagements, deviant dress patterns in non-June brides, and household hints for the have-nots.

She was delighted, thrilled, and thought everything was "darling." It was the first time, she said, that she had ever been in a real artist's studio. She took off her gloves, her hat and her coat. And sat on the cat.

I offered Band-Aids, but she wouldn't let me look. The interview was somewhat shorter than I expected, and so was the piece in the paper. She called my dish African Chicken. I suppose it's hard to get things correct when you're standing up to type.

Toss a cut up chicken in 1 tsp salt, 1 tsp turmeric and 1 tsp powdered ginger. Quick fry chicken and 1 sliced onion in 2 Tbsp oil over high heat, 1 minute on each side. Add 3 Tbsp peanut butter, 2 cut up tomatoes, ½ c water, ½ tsp nutmeg, 1 tsp ginger, ½ tsp pepper, ¼ tsp cayenne and ½ tsp tomato paste. Take out chicken, dust with grated coconut and set aside, leaving sauce in the pan. Add any mixture of cut up vegetables in sauce, stir and cook 20 minutes. Salt if desired.

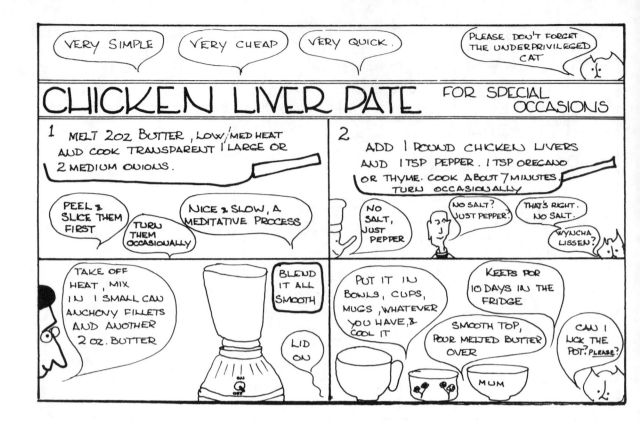

Chicken Liver Paté

In junk stores you can find cups, or little bowls, souvenirs of somebody's honeymoon, of trips to Disneyland or even, as my favourite mug proudly proclaims, "Presented by The Women's Credit Managers Breakfast Club for Perfect Attendance." There are honey pots, old mustard pots, marmalade jars, even odd wine glasses. If you don't insist on a set, or a matching saucer, you can pick them up for less than a dollar.

Then you can fill them with chicken liver paté, carefully pour butter over the top, tidy up any splashes, and have a perfectly acceptable Christmas present. If you want to make it bigger, wrap a box of crackers too, the whole tied up with ribbon.

This is the only recipe in the book that calls for special equipment. If you don't have a blender, mash the pate as smooth as you can with a fork—the butter will smooth it all out. And why no salt? Well, as all Jewish grandmothers know, salt makes the edges go dark. Sprinkle on a little salt when it's actually on the cracker.

Melt 2 oz butter over low-medium heat and cook slowly until transparent 1 large or 2 medium onions, sliced. Add 1 lb chicken livers, 1 tsp pepper, 1 tsp oregano or thyme. Cook about 7 minutes, turning occasionally. Remove pan from heat, mix in 1 small can anchovy fillets and another 2 oz butter. Blend until smooth. Scrape into small bowls or cups, pour melted butter over top and cool. Keeps refrigerated for 10 days.

Dinner in 20 Minutes If You Hurry, 25 If You Don't

Art was once a snob's private park. I used to be told that I couldn't paint or draw. I used to be taken to museums and shown what *real* art was, and most of the time I was too terrified to even try to understand what I was seeing.

Food used to be almost the same experience. It couldn't be fun, it had to be serious, and you had to know all the names, preferably in a foreign language.

Then I discovered that the French made food, and made love, in their own language. They cooked because they were hungry, and they made love because they were passionate. We had it all confused: if we weren't doing it with a French accent it was meaningless, and a whole race of gourmets squeezed itself into *la cuisine and l'amour.* If Charles Boyer had had an American accent, he could never have said, "Come wiz me to ze Kasbah..."

If you let your gourmet friends get at this dish, they will call it *Poulet Bonne Femme,* which to the French means almost anything with potatoes, a bit of bacon and some peas in it. Traditionally they use salt pork if they've got it, and so can you. But while your high-class friends are desperately shopping all over town for snob ingredients, you and your simpler friends are sitting down to supper, getting into the second bottle of wine, and maybe commenting on the fact that eating is, first of all, fun.

Chop 4 slices bacon and fry over medium-high heat until there is some fat in the pan. Dice 2 medium potatoes and stir-fry them with the bacon, just until they change color. Take everything out of the pan, except the fat, turn the heat up to high and fry 6 or 8 chicken wings for 1 minute on each side. Add 1 medium onion and 1 clove garlic, chopped, 1 c water, 1 large cut up tomato, 1 heaping tsp thyme, 1 tsp salt and ½ tsp pepper. Return potatoes and bacon to pan and cook over low heat, covered, for 10 minutes. Add 1 packet frozen peas and cook, covered, for 5 minutes.

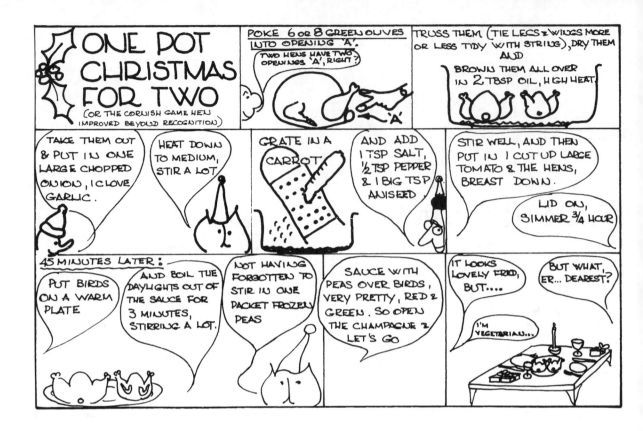

One-Pot Christmas for Two

Rock Cornish game hens are one of Nature's drearier mistakes. Almost as though she had decided to make it up to chickens for being so stupid and asked a television studio to dream up a glamorous, pocket-sized image for them to aspire to.

I've got nothing against Gidget, except that she's dull, dim-witted and sexless, a victim of an advertising department's puffed up prose. And that's what I've got against Rock Cornish game hens— they pop up in all sorts of fancy (and not so fancy) places, accompanied by unbelievable prose: "Pit bred fighting bantams at the peak of condition, oven-roased in their own succulent juices and served at your table with our fabulous French Fries fried (in France) in a French French-fryer..."

Rock Cornish game hens have no natural juices. What you usually end up with is a dried up dwarf bird cowering in shame beneath a varnish of brown wallpaper paste. Small frozen birds (it sounds sad but that's what these are) need moist cooking (like most ducks) and their juices need supplementing with onions and garlic and the more fragrant spices. There should be enough juice in the tomato and onion to make a sauce, but if you want to put in a glass of red wine, go ahead.

What comes out of this pot is a joy and delight, a particularly good Christmas dish, one bird apiece, fingers to lick, no oven to clean, no fuss, and a good smell everywhere. Two-people Christmases are the ones you remember for a long time.

Stuff 2 Cornish game hens with 6 or 8 green olives, truss them, dry them and brown them in 2 Tbsp oil over high heat. Remove the birds from the pan and stir into oil 1 large chopped onion and 1 clove garlic. Reduce heat to medium and stir. Grate into pan 1 carrot and add 1 tsp salt, ½ tsp pepper and 1 rounded tsp aniseed. Stir well, then add 1 large cut up tomato and the hens, breast down. Cover and simmer ¾ hour. Place birds on a warm plate, add 1 packet of frozen peas and boil sauce hard for 3 minutes, stirring constantly. Serve sauce over birds.

Coq au Vin

When the autumn leaves start to fall chickens are cheap. Not the little, skinny mini-skirted spring chickens, but the tough old heavies who just can't make it any more in the egg parlours. They call them Grade B, and they sell for about forty cents a pound.

While you are shopping, pick up half a pound of small onions. Really small ones, little round pretty ones. And about a quarter pound of meaty back bacon. If you're short of money get bacon ends and cut off the fat. And a bottle of half decent burgundy. The better the wine, the better the dish. Don't, unless you are a confirmed masochist, use Rubby Reds for cooking. And get a bunch of parsley. Keep what you don't use in a plastic bag in the refrigerator. A loaf of French bread is also timely.

Now, accept the fact that it's easy. Place two or three ounces of butter in the heavy iron frying pan, and brown the chicken (which of course you have defrosted) all over. Put it aside in a warm place—the oven if you want, very low, and brown the onions (whole) and the bacon (in strips) in the same pan. While the onions are browning, joint the chicken—wings, legs, and the carcass—into four pieces. Put it all together in the pan, turn the heat up high and add half the wine. Have a glass for yourself while you are at it. Crush a clove of garlic, put that in, and a little salt. The rest of the salt goes in when you are ready to serve. A little pepper, and a bouquet garni. Put the lid on, turn down the heat to very slow, and leave it for about a few hours. Take a book and another glass of wine to the bath, with a note on the door, if you are a mother, to say that you are cooking dinner and must not be disturbed.

In three hours or so (time is not important) it will be ready. Take out the bouquet garni, thicken the pot a little with *beurre manié*, add a little salt to taste, and brown the sliced bread in butter or cooking oil (not olive oil this time). Put the chicken on the table, liberally sprinkled with chopped parsley.

Serve it with the bread, and green peas, and rice, or mashed potatoes. That's it—Coq au Vin, a French name for a simple dish.

A bouquet garni is a bunch of parsley stalks

continued

(keep the leaves for the final serving). Tie the stalks in a bunch with a bay leaf, and a sprig of thyme, and leave a long end on the string so that you can find it later. If you can't find fresh herbs, use Spice Islands bottled bouquet garni tied up in muslin, and if you can't be bothered with the muslin, just dump it in the pot. It tastes the same, but looks better with the little extra care.

Beurre manié is a mixture of butter and flour. About twice as much butter as flour. Mix it together into a paste and roll it into little balls, about a quarter of an inch across. To thicken, add the balls one or two at a time to the pan until it is thick enough. Shake, not stir, because the stirring will break up the meat. Bring to the boil, and that's it. *Bon Appetit.*

Slowly brown an old chicken in butter. Take out chicken and keep warm. Brown ½ lb small chopped onions and ½ lb chopped bacon in pan. Joint the chicken, add to pan with onions and bacon, turn up heat to high and add ½ bottle decent red wine. Add a few sprigs parsley, 1 sprig thyme and 1 bay leaf, all bundled together, 1 crushed clove garlic and a small amount of salt and pepper (don't salt to taste at this stage). Cover, lower heat and simmer slowly for at least 3 hours. Take out herb bundle. To thicken stew mix into a paste, then into little balls, 2 parts butter to every 1 part flour. Add the balls to the stew until it is slightly thickened. Salt stew to taste. Serve with croutons made of cubed French bread browned in cooking oil.

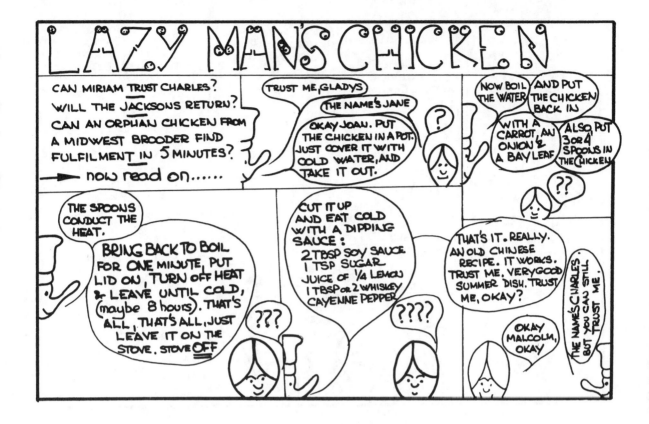

Lazy Man's Chicken

Everybody knows about Archimedes jumping out of his bath and rushing naked up the main street of Syracuse when he first figured out the law of flotation.

But history books are strangely silent upon his second discovery, which was how to cook a chicken with hardly any work and almost no energy.

Which I now, in the humility becoming a classical scholar, present to you, without subsidy from any major (or minor) institute of learning. I also take the opportunity to thank my mother, who is still wondering whether or not all that education was worthwhile, and consistently urges me to take up a respectable profession, preferably one that requires the wearing of a suit to an office, and certainly one that offers a regular paycheque.

You can't go wrong with this. You don't even have to use a whole chicken; it works with chicken breasts (of course, they have no hole to put the spoons in) or whatever assorted pieces you care to collect from the butcher. The timing is for a whole chicken; however, if it's pieces you are using, add just a little more water. You can throw an onion in too, cut up a bit, and a carrot. Keep the broth; it makes a good soup base for next day. Or you can hot it up for a preface to the chicken dinner, salt it a little, throw in a handful of finely chopped fresh vegetables, almost anything such as a tomato or some leeks, some pasta if you have it—but what comes out will be chicken soup. Presto, you're a Jewish mother.

Place a chicken in a pot, pour in water just to cover chicken and immediately remove chicken. Put 3 or 4 spoons inside chicken to conduct heat. Boil the water, put chicken (with spoons inside) back in the pot with 1 carrot, 1 peeled onion and 1 bay leaf. Boil for 1 minute, cover pot, turn off heat and leave until cold, about 8 hours. Eat chicken cold with a mixture of 2 Tbsp soy sauce, 1 tsp sugar, juice of ¼ lemon OR 1 or 2 Tbsp whiskey, and a dash of cayenne pepper.

Piccata di Vitello

James, will you marry me?

I had never been proposed to by a man before. It was the end of my first television show. In fourteen minutes (because rice takes that long to cook) with Peter Gzowski (who was no Johnny Carson), we had made a whole dinner, all of it on a two-burner pump-up stove. We had soup, and this Piccata di Vitello, and asparagus, and the rice bright yellow and delightful, and dessert, and coffee. And we got hundreds of letters.

We had never cooked together before, there was no rehearsal, no back-up kitchen, no special facilities—just a Coleman camp stove, a fry pan, a coffee pot (in which we cooked the coffee and asparagus) and a little saucepan for the soup.

The recipe in the drawing uses chicken breasts because they are cheaper than veal. I use veal because that is the classic basis of this dish, and there is a special marriage between veal, butter and lemon, something super-rich. It is the sort of dish that only the very best of restaurants would dare serve because it is so simple, like most of the great secrets of the world.

If you want to tart it up a little, throw in a hand-

ful of smallish mushrooms (the white ones, cut in half) when the white wine goes in. And if you want to make the rice a colour spectacular, throw a teaspoon of turmeric (very cheap, not like saffron) into the water and stir in a handful of very finely cut green onions just before you serve it.

Flour 2 boned chicken breasts and pound thin between waxed paper. Heat 2 or 3 Tbsp butter over medium heat until frothy and cook chicken breasts until the edges go white, about 2 minutes on each side. Salt chicken lightly and add ¼ bottle dry white wine. Cook about 2 minutes more. Sprinkle chicken with juice of ½ lemon. Take out chicken and boil down sauce vigorously, about 30 seconds. Pour sauce over chicken and serve immediately.

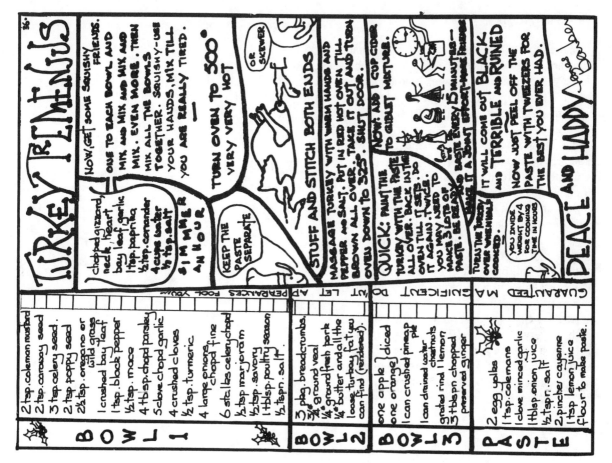

Turkey Tremenjus

There is just no way to describe this turkey, other than the friendliest cooking you will ever experience. I mean, you need friends for a turkey, just to eat it, so you might as well get them there early and spend the day doing it.

We sit around and drink a bit, lie a bit and dream a bit. Somebody gets up to look at it, or baste it, or just smell it, every fifteen minutes or so, and people go for walks and get hungry, or play with whatever the kids got for Christmas.

It looks really terrible. The first time I tried it I was most ashamed—everybody's dinner was ruined and I was going to write letters to the newspaper I got it from, and Pierre Berton and Himie Koshevoy—and all the other people who had recommended it—but we all kept basting and sipping and finally we fished it out and did what the book says. It was magnificent, like a twenty-pound pheasant. Get one between eighteen and twenty-two pounds, and a dozen or so friends. Happy Christmas, or Thanksgiving, or whenever you decide to do it.

In a bowl combine 2 tsp Coleman mustard, 2 tsp caraway seed, 3 tsp celery seed, 2 tsp poppy seed, 2½ tsp oregano or wild grass, 1 crushed bay leaf, 1 tsp black pepper, ½ tsp mace, 4 Tbsp chopped parsley, 5 cloves chopped garlic, 4 crushed cloves, ½ tsp turmeric, 4 large finely chopped onions, 6 stalks chopped celery, ½ tsp marjoram, ½ tsp poultry seasoning and ½ tsp salt. Mix thoroughly.

In another bowl combine 3 pkg breadcrumbs, ¾ lb ground veal, ¼ lb ground fresh pork, ¼ lb butter and as much rendered turkey fat as available. Mix thoroughly.

In another bowl combine 1 diced apple, 1 diced orange, 1 can crushed pineapple, 1 can drained water chestnuts, grated rind of 1 lemon and 3 Tbsp chopped preserved ginger. Mix thoroughly.

continued

Turkey Tremenjus

Make a paste of 2 egg yolks, 1 tsp Coleman mustard, 1 clove minced garlic, 1 Tbsp onion juice, ½ tsp salt, 2 pinches cayenne, 1 tsp lemon juice and enough flour to make a paste.

Combine in a pot and simmer 1 hour: chopped turkey gizzard, neck and heart, a bay leaf, 1 garlic clove, 1 tsp paprika, ½ tsp coriander, 4 c water and ½ tsp salt.

Combine ingredients of all three bowls (but not the paste) and mix thoroughly. Stuff mixture in turkey and stitch closed at both ends. Massage outside of turkey with salt and pepper, put in a 500 degree oven and brown all over. Remove turkey and turn oven down to 325 degrees. Paint turkey with paste and put back in oven until paste sets. Paint turkey again with paste (make more paste if necessary).

Add 1 c cider to giblet mixture and baste turkey with it every 15 minutes. Turn turkey when half cooked, and baste and cook on other side. Divide weight of turkey by 4 to get hours cooking time. Turkey should turn black when done. Remove paste and serve.

Eight Hour Chicken

Forget all the brainwashing about high temperatures, about 450 degrees for an hour then exactly 400 for twenty minutes. And at the same time forget all about the expensive cuts of meat, except for very special occasions. Forget also about TV dinners, or hurried hamburgers. Just get up, put the chicken in the oven, and forget about it. If your oven will set at lower than 200 degrees, then set it there, somewhere around 175 if you can, and then forget it for even longer.

You can, at the same time, forget all about cleaning the oven, because with low temperature cooking there is not fat splashing around, just a gentle, warm comfortable happening.

Try it first with a cheap chicken. Come home, put some rice or potatoes on the fire. Put a few instant onions or chopped onions in with the rice if you like, and a little bit of butter, and five minutes before it is cooked a few frozen peas. Sprinkle a little curry powder on the rice, and there's dinner, the inside of the chicken filled with juice which also is nice on the rice, and the meat moist and tender. Some ovens turn the skin into a brittle, parchment-like affair which you just discard, others get it brown and crispy.

Sometimes I cover the pan loosely with foil (don't tuck it in) and sometimes I just leave things as they are. The most successful meal I have ever cooked this way was one evening or early morning when I came home drunk, got into bed, and remembered I had guests coming for lunch. I crawled out of bed, pulled the chicken out of the fridge, and managed, at the third attempt, to get it into the frying pan. And the frying pan, at the fourth attempt, into the oven. There it lay, until my guests woke me next day. They were very smug, but not half as smug as I was when twenty minutes after they arrived they were sitting down to roast chicken.

This is a technique which will teach you to cook. You make your own mind up about what you like best, make notes, and almost anything you do will be right. Eight hours, ten hours, it doesn't really matter.

Try it with cheap frozen lamb rubbed with oregano and garlic. Get a cheap roast of pork and

continued

treat it to lots of basil and a little pepper and salt.
Get a cross rib roast, massage it with garlic and
pepper and salt. Get an old duck, or a real monster
of an old goose which has to be cheap, poke an
onion or two inside and maybe an orange. Forget
it. Don't worry. Write a book. Teach yourself to
crochet. Learn Japanese, lift weights, even
meditate.

But forget the dinner until you are ready.

Rub salt and pepper into an old chicken. Cover
chicken loosely with foil and place in a pan. Cook
in a 200 degree oven for at least 8 hours. Pour
juices from foil into a pan, add ½ finely chopped
onion and some wine or water. Simmer 5 minutes.
Add ¼ pt cream and salt and pepper to taste.
Serve sauce over chicken.

Huevos Rancheros

Brunch is disaster. We've all been sucked in by the *House and Garden* photographs of beautiful people, at ease in their caftans, leisure suits and ear-to-ear smiles, while host and hostess graciously dispense Tequila Sunrises.

Brunch in fact leads to divorce. Nobody wants to be settled for life with somebody offering rubber eggs, cardboard bacon, apathetic toast and tired coffee. Eggs Benedict, that staple of bourgeois brunches, usually ends in total disaster, harsh words in the kitchen, the guests leaving early and saying much too brightly, "How marvellous, darling, how terribly clever of you." And even before the car door is closed one of them says, "Let's not send *them* a Christmas card."

This is a no-nonsense brunch, eminently suitable for a very limited kitchen. You can make the sauce the night before and with a good big pan you can cook eight eggs at a time.

And what goes best with Huevos Rancheros is beer. Mexican beer is best, and that's how I first ate it, dreadfully hung over one morning in Santo Tomás, a long cold beer before, one with and two or three afterwards, while we watched, on the other side of the road, a man quietly and competently shave a twenty-foot pole into long slivers, which he then made into a basket and sold for a dollar, after which he got on his horse and rode off.

If you have a spare green pepper, slice it thin and put it in the sauce. You can then call it Piperade, and pretend you are in the South of France.

Chop fine 1 large onion, 1 clove garlic and 4 large tomatoes. Mix until smooth with a small amount of water, 2 tsp flour, 4 tsp chili powder, 1 tsp mint, 1 tsp sage, 1 tsp salt and 2 Tbsp tomato paste. Cook onion and garlic in 2 Tbsp oil over medium heat until they are transparent. Add tomatoes and cook 5 minutes, stirring. Add spices and 2 c water. Simmer 20 minutes, stirring frequently. Add more water if the mixture gets too thick. Crack 2 eggs for each person into a saucer and slide them into pan. Poach eggs until the whites set.

Oeufs Florentine

The French muck spinach about, they put cream in it and they grind it into baby food, they alter it and change it, beat it and butter it, until finally there is nothing of spinach about it, no green-leafed sunshine. It is nothing that grew in a garden and children looked at, nothing that a woman seven months pregnant might have picked for her man as a memory of the green grass they made the baby on.

Only the Japanese and the Italians understand spinach. Raw in a salad, with lemon juice, olive oil, a little green dill and a finely chopped hard-boiled egg: that's okay, that's America's understanding of it, it's healthy and it's horny.

But most of the gourmet books insist that it be boiled into submission.

Ouefs Florentine is a gentle, soul-warming dish, very quick and easy, a perfect light lunch but an even better prescription for those dreadful days when nobody loves you and you feel like a Billie Holiday LP—"I Gotta Right to Sing the Blues...."

For a marvellous and unusual cold vegetable (which you can make the night before, or a couple of hours before) cook the spinach, drain it well in a colander, and shape it into long rolls about an inch in diameter. Sprinkle soy sauce on the rolls, then slice them carefully into pieces about an inch long (that way each is a mouthful), arrange prettily on a simple white plate, and let cool in the fridge for a while. Enjoy.

Prepare frozen spinach, cooking only half the time indicated on packet, OR wash fresh spinach well in salt water, shake dry and cook 5 minutes without water with pan lid on. Break eggs into a saucer. Add 1 Tbsp vinegar to boiling water in a saucepan, spin water around with spoon and slip eggs into the middle. When eggs are poached, remove them with a slotted spoon, place on hot drained spinach, butter and sprinkle with paprika.

Risotto Milanese

The simplest of all dishes. A care-and-nurturing recipe. A kind dinner. There is a hypnotic quality to the slow and careful turning. None of this frantic dabbing, like an old lady with an umbrella trying to get a cow out of the garden, but a considerate, loving, Strauss waltz round and rounding.

The more care you put into it, the more velvety the result. It is indeed remarkable, the sort of dish that is so simple to learn and so disproportionately productive of a reputation. You will never again be forced back to that tired old lasagna recipe that everybody has.

Fry until golden 1 medium onion chopped very fine in 2 oz butter over medium heat. Add 1 c uncooked rice and turn until it glistens. Add 1 can beef bouillon OR chicken stock slowly, ½ tsp pepper and 1 tsp salt. Turn rice mixture until the stock is absorbed. Add 1 can of water gradually. Soak a few strands of saffron in a small amount of hot water, then pour it into rice. Add 4 Tbsp grated parmesan as soon as the rice is tender.

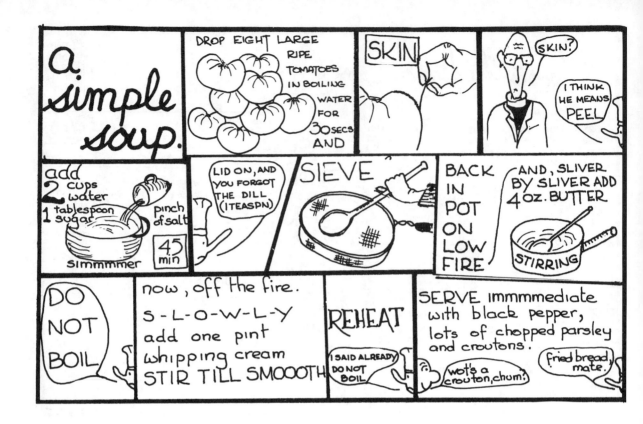

A Simple Soup

This is a fall soup, a special for someone you specially want to please. Tomatoes are cheap in the fall, and it is not really a very expensive soup, but is almost obscenely luxurious, a smooth, soft, gentle, fattening, rich thing which makes a very pleasant light supper, particularly by the fire and with, if you can find it, a bottle of that Portuguese green wine very cold.

The important thing is not to boil it, or it will curdle. Gentle it all the way through, gentle in the butter in slivers, stirring all the time, and gentle in the cream, stirring all the time. It should be a pleasant, soft sensation, and once you have started adding things, keep the heat soft and gentle. If you let it boil it will curdle, so be nice to it.

Croutons are just cubes of oldish bread, warmed, rather than fried, very slowly in lots of butter. I usually do them in the oven in my big iron frying pan. Melt the butter, toss the cubes in it until they are coated, add a chopped clove of garlic if you wish, or a couple of handfuls of chopped parsley, and put them in a low oven (250 degrees) for an hour or so. Let them cool, and keep in a screw-top jar and use in soups and salads, or just eat them with a glass of wine while you wait for dinner to cook.

And don't forget the dill. If you haven't got any, get some, and start using it on all sorts of things. Cook beets in it, sprinkle it on fish, especially shellfish, and even if you have to finish up one day with a can of soup, throw in a little dill and surprise yourself. Canned tomato soup with dill in it tastes almost as good as the advertisements say it does.

Drop 8 large ripe tomatoes in boiling water for 30 seconds and peel. Add 2 c water, 1 Tbsp sugar, a pinch of salt and 1 tsp dill. Simmer, covered, 45 minutes. Strain soup and return to pot over low heat, adding 4 oz butter in small slivers. Do not boil. Take off heat and add 1 pt whipping cream gradually, stirring until smooth. Reheat, but do not boil. Serve hot with black pepper and chopped parsley and croutons.

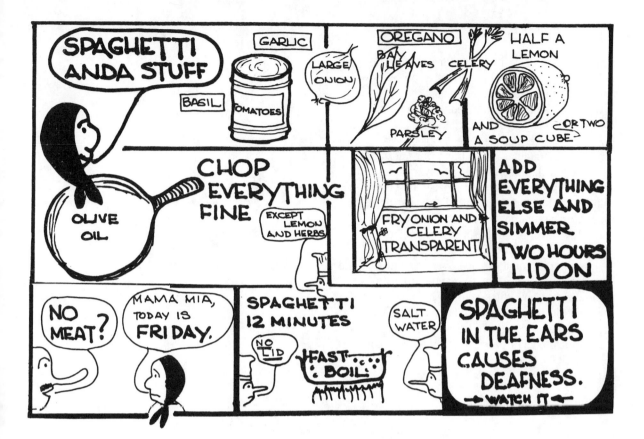

Spaghetti anda Stuff

Just cook it long enough—and slowly. What you don't eat, put in little plastic bags and place in the freezer of your refrigerator.

It's a tomato sauce, originally for lasagna. If you want to stiffen it up in a hurry, fry half a pound of hamburger until it separates, then pour on the sauce and cook together for half an hour.

If you want it even thicker, add tomato paste. Canned tomatoes are better and cheaper for spaghetti than most fresh ones. If you do use fresh ones, skin them first by putting them in boiling water for a couple of minutes. The skin will peel off easily.

The lemon is important. Take it out before you store the sauce. Use lots of basil, at least a teaspoonful, and half as much oregano.

Now we come to the serious business. There are two tests of true love in the kitchen. One is making Eggs Benedict, the other is fresh pasta, or "pasta fatta in casa." It takes time, so do it on a rainy Saturday. Cook it while the sauce is on the fire.

Spaghetti, lasagna, macaroni and rigatoni,

they're all the same stuff—pasta. And there is no taste in the world like a lasagna made with fresh pasta. So. Lasagna *al forno*.

3 eggs, well beaten.
small teaspoon salt.
1 pound flour.
5 tablespoons water.

Mix it soft to a ball. You might need a little more water. Sprinkle a board with flour and knead the dough for about fifteen minutes with the heel of your hand. Sprinkle a little flour around occasionally so it won't stick.

It's a nice time to talk to people. That's why good bread-makers become such nice people.

Twist the dough off into six parts. One at a time, put them on a board and roll them as thin as you can. I use a wine bottle for a rolling pin. Sprinkle a bit more flour about. It's very elastic, so it's hard work.

Fold it over a couple of times, and do it over again. Three times. For lasagna, cut the final thin dough into two-inch strips, and put them some-

continued

where on a clean cloth to dry for about an hour.

The sauce is beginning to smell good by now and might need half a cup of water.

Now. Homemade pasta needs only half as much cooking time as the commercial kind. Lots of boiling salted water, and cook the strips of lasagna three to four minutes. Take them out and drain.

Butter a dish (lots of butter), a layer of cooked lasagna, a layer of crumbled mozzarella cheese, a thin layer of either chopped Italian sausage, or salami, or hamburger rolled into little balls.

Another layer of thinly sliced hardboiled eggs, and sprinkle it all with Parmesan cheese.

Now the thin tomato sauce over all, and start the layers all over again—twice, maybe three times, depending on how thick your pasta is.

Finish top with tomato sauce and a few knobs of butter. Bake at 350 to 375 degrees for half an hour.

If you use bought pasta, that's okay. But boil it ten minutes.

Chop 1 garlic, 1 large can tomatoes and 2 stalks celery. Fry onions and celery in olive oil. Add 1 tsp basil, 2 bay leaves, 1 pinch parsley, 1 lemon and 1 or 2 bouillon cubes. Simmer, covered, 2 hours. Serve as suggested above.

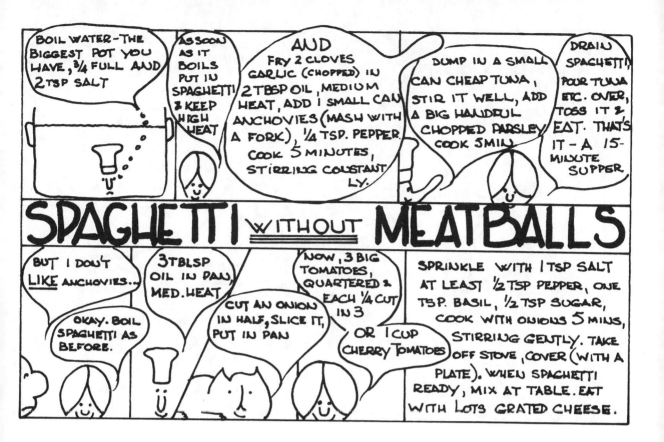

Spaghetti Without Meatballs

Agnolotti, bucatini, capellini, cappelletti—there are thousands of shapes and sizes of pasta, and hundreds of different ways of cooking each one. But nobody in North America seems to know that, so we settle for lasagna, spaghetti and meatballs, or, for the the truly adventurous, spaghetti with clam sauce.

Time to try something else. You don't have to have meat, and once you get used to the idea of making a quick sauce—just a frypan and a little oil with whatever's at hand—you're half way to becoming really Italian.

And then you can think of uncooked sauces. Around Naples they chop fresh tomatoes, some garlic, a little basil, and marinate it all in a quarter cup of olive oil (and of course the tomato juices). If they haven't got basil they use oregano, and so can you. Thyme is okay, too, or marjoram. Marinating means letting everything sit, a couple of hours or all day while you're at work. Come home, cook the pasta, drain it, dump the tomatoes and oil on, toss it all and eat immediately.

Don't ever cook pasta before guests come; it's worth making them wait. And if you've got any pasta left over, toss it with a little olive oil, a little lemon juice and perhaps half a teaspoon of salt. A bit of finely chopped onion, some parsley, and next day (after it sits in the fridge all night) you've got a wonderful cold salad.

Boil spaghetti with 2 Tbsp salt in a large pan. Fry 2 cloves chopped garlic over medium heat in 2 Tbsp oil. Add 1 small can anchovies, mashed, and ¼ tsp pepper. Cook 5 minutes, stirring constantly. Add 1 small can tuna, stir well, and add 1 large handful chopped parsley. Toss tuna mixture with cooked, drained spaghetti. OR cook ½ sliced onion in 3 Tbsp oil. Add 3 large quartered tomatoes OR 1 c cherry tomatoes. Sprinkle with 1 tsp salt, ½ tsp pepper, 1 tsp basil and ½ tsp sugar and cook with onions for 5 minutes, stirring gently. Mix sauce with spaghetti at table and serve with cheese.

Tortilla Española

Hot, cold or lukewarm, the Spanish tortilla (which has nothing at all to do with the Mexican tortilla) is always good. Spanish women are known for their tortillas, in much the same way as, a few years ago, country women were known for their cakes. The simplest of all, with potatoes, is a great favorite in tapas bars, served cold in wedges with rich, rough red wines. Once you have mastered the art (much of which lies in flipping the tortilla over with the plate) then you can experiment on your own, because basically this is a country dish, not a haute cuisine gourmet number, and it makes use of whatever is around. By the time you've tried a little broccoli in it, or maybe some spinach, it probably will have evolved into an Italian frittata, and with a little chopped bacon it gets to be a Denver sandwich. But it's cheap, and it's quick, and it keeps—the ideal quick dish with which to impress visitors and still have a bit left over for the next day.

Peel and dice into ½-inch cubes 1 medium potato. Peel and chop 1 medium onion. Combine potato and onion and fry in 3 Tbsp olive oil over medium heat, stirring frequently. Beat 5 eggs lightly with 1 tsp salt and ½ tsp pepper. When potatoes are just tender (about 10 minutes) pour eggs over and lower heat. Cover and cook until top is firm (about 10 minutes. Turn pan over (so tortilla drops on to plate) and slide back into pan. Cook 2 minutes more, uncovered. See alternative ingredients above.

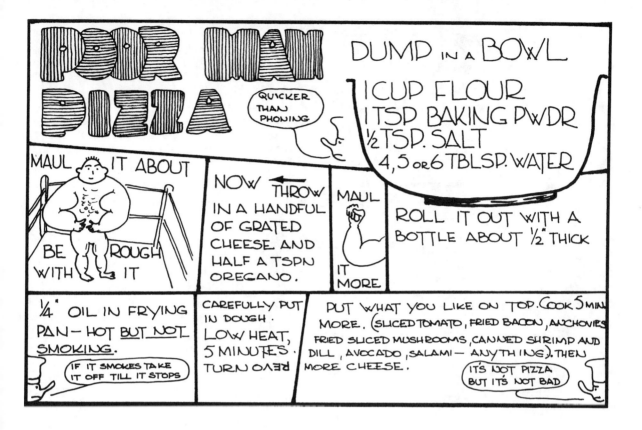

Poor Man Pizza

If you live in a basement suite with a fire-breathing landlady who doesn't want you to cook, to come in late, to have visitors after 10:00 p.m., smoke, drink, bath more than once a week or turn over in bed because it wears out the sheets, then you have a problem.

This recipe is specifically for basement suite dwellers who hide the hotplate and the frying pan under the bed. It can be made by others, by children for supper, and by hungry drunks as a measure of their sobriety, by diesel mechanics wishing to get their fingernails clean and by the totally incompetent who normally manage to mess up the preparation of something so simple as a can of sardines.

It is simple, and foolproof. Nothing you can do to the dough can spoil it. It is indigestible, filling, and as interesting as you care to make it.

The only care that must be taken is in the frying. The oil must be hot, but not smoking, so that after five minutes cooking the underside is a golden brown, not too hard but just crisp. It is so cheap to make that if you foul it up you just throw it away,

feed it to the dog, or keep it till next morning as a special treat for the seagulls on the beach.

Combine 1 c flour, 1 tsp baking powder, ½ tsp salt and 4 to 6 Tbsp water. Knead, then add in a handful of grated cheese and ½ tsp oregano. Knead and roll out ½-inch thick. Pour ¼-inch oil in a frying pan and heat hot but not smoking. Carefully put in dough, lower heat and cook 5 minutes. Turn over. Top with desired ingredients, cook 5 minutes and sprinkle with more cheese.

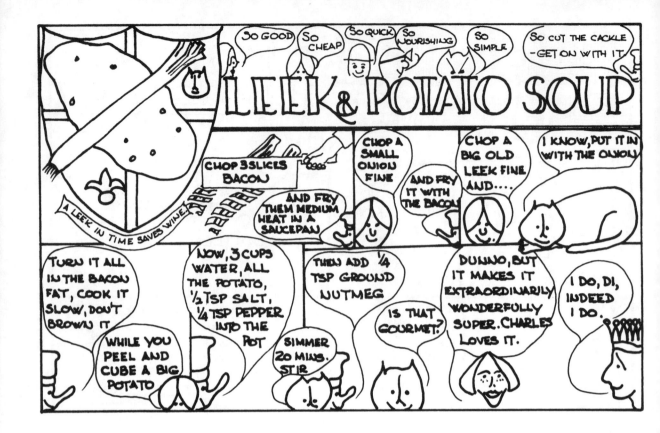

Leek and Potato Soup

This is really where this book started. It was November and raining and Sunday and sad. There were three of us in a cottage. Pictures of the cottage in summer showed roses round the door, thatch on the roof and an unmistakable air of English countryside curling over the picket fence. The reality of it in winter was mud to the doorstep, damp from floor to ceiling, no electricity, mice in the walls and the only form of heat a fireplace that smoked into the house instead of out.

We made this soup without leeks from onions we found in a shed. We had half a garlic sausage left over from Saturday's picnic, and there were potatoes with the onions. It was wonderful. Tiredness and hunger will always spice up the plainest dish.

You can make this soup from almost anything. Leeks are nice but not absolutely necessary. A bit of leftover ham works instead of bacon, and if you don't put in any meat at all but add a half cup of cream two minutes before serving, it's still delicious. Put it through a blender and chill it for vichyssoise; or mash it a bit with a wooden spoon (the way I like it, just a little lumpy) and it has a

simple homemade innocence about it.

The essential ingredient is the nutmeg, which mice don't appear to like. I'm not suggesting nutmeg as a mouse repellent, but I am insisting on it for this soup or any variations of it. Nutmeg is a great spice to have around; it transforms the dullness of cauliflower, it makes rice pudding attractive even to five-year-olds, and of course it is basic to hot winter drinks. Try a bit sprinkled on warmed (not boiled) beer, with a little lemon juice added and a spoonful of sugar. Sensational.

Chop 3 slices bacon and fry over medium heat. Chop 1 small onion fine and fry it with the bacon. Chop 1 large old leek fine and add to the pan, stirring over low heat (do not allow to brown). Peel and cube 1 large potato. Add 3 c water, the potato, ½ tsp salt and ¼ tsp pepper to the pan and simmer 20 minutes, stirring often. Add ¼ tsp ground nutmeg and serve.

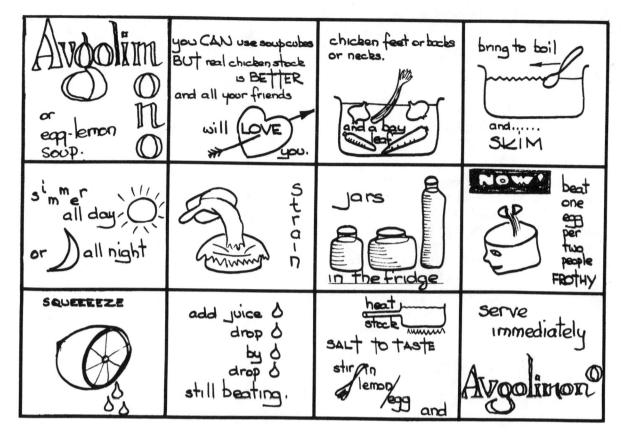

The illustrated recipe panels read:

Avgolimono or egg-lemon soup.

you CAN use soup cubes BUT real chicken stock is BETTER and all your friends will LOVE you.

chicken feet or backs or necks. and a bay leaf

bring to boil and...... SKIM

simmer all day or all night

Strain

Jars in the fridge

NOW! beat one egg per two people FROTHY

SQUEEEEZE

add juice drop by drop still beating.

heat stock SALT to TASTE stir in lemon/egg and

serve immediately Avgolimono

Avgolimono

Avgolimono is one of the smoothest, most delightful, and most surprising little soups I know. It is a little soup, not a great knife and fork effort or a cream soup with extra pans to wash, but just a simple little soup that tastes great, is elegant enough for anybody's dinner table, and gentle enough to be much appreciated during or after the flu.

Once you know how to make it you'll be able to do it with your eyes closed.

1. Hot chicken soup. I make my own, but cubes will work almost as well.

2. One egg for two people. Beat it well, until it's frothy and light.

3. Half a lemon per egg. Squeeze the juice very slowly, drop by drop, into the egg. Keep beating.

4. Have bowls ready. Pour the egg lemon mixture into the soup. Keep beating. Don't boil it, just put it in and keep beating for thirty seconds. Take it off the stove, and serve.

It's a lovely colour, very good on a fall day.

Now, the serious business of chicken stock. I buy chicken feet in Chinatown on Saturday mornings. Or I buy chicken necks and backs at the butcher shop. All of which are very cheap. Take them home, dump them in a big pot, and cover with water. A veal knuckle is nice too, but it isn't essential. Put in a couple of onions, and carrots, a stick or two of celery. A bay leaf and just a pinch of salt. You can add more salt when things are done, but just a little right now does things for the vegetable flavours. Bring it to a boil, and turn heat down to simmer. Five minutes later, skim it with a spoon. If you get all the foam off the top the final stock will be clear.

Put the lid on tight, and simmer for a long time. I let mine do it all night and get up in the morning to memories of my grandmother. Strain it, and put it in jars, and use it for lots of things. Throw away the vegetables, and if you want a nice, messy job take the meat off the chicken necks with your fingers.

Some fresh vegetables, sliced fine, some of the stock, a little salt and pepper and fifteen minutes cooking will make a good lunch with fresh bread.

The stock will jell in the fridge. Use it as you

continued

would soup cubes, for Chinese food, stews, for cooking cabbage and peas, for making spaghetti sauce, or borscht.

Make a chicken stock or dissolve chicken cubes in water. Add 1 stalk chopped celery, 2 chopped carrots, 2 chopped onions and 1 bay leaf. Bring to a boil and skim. Simmer all day or all night, strain into jars and refrigerate. Beat 1 egg for each 2 people. Add juice of lemon, one drop at a time, to egg mixture, beating the eggs with each addition. Heat stock and salt to taste. Stir in lemon and egg mixture and serve immediately.

Omelette

Put anything in this omelette, like grated cheese, or honey, or mushrooms sliced and gently fried in butter with basil, or shrimps or crabs with dill, or caviar (the cheap kind is enough and it's a fantastic Sunday breakfast) or tomatoes and onions sliced and fried with a little olive oil and some oregano or crumbled bacon or parsley or some just fried beans sprouts with a little onion and a crushed flower of star anise.

And if you want to make a lunch of it, most elegant, make borscht first, preferably the day before. Get two bunches of fresh beets, cut off tops and bottoms, slice them, put in about a quart and a half of water, a teaspoonful of dill, a pinch of salt and a teaspoonful of sugar.

Boil them all for an hour. Strain, put the beets in vinegar to eat later with cheese, and put the soup (it's purple and looks like good wine) in the refrigerator. Serve cold, with lots of sour cream and chopped cucumber (skin on). Very good with Portuguese Vinho Verde.

Do it with style, and let it take five minutes. Borscht in the bowls, sour cream ready, cucumber chopped. Then quick, beat the eggs, six for two of you, nine for three, but cook them three at a time. Most soup ladles hold exactly three beaten eggs.

Heat the pan (keep the flame high) until water flicked on it bounces. Dump in the butter and swish it around until it foams (but don't let it get brown). Quick with the first three eggs, and immediately stir with the fork flat on the bottom of the pan. Vigorously. Until the eggs are just set. Then you have a minute.

Leave the pan to sit, put in the filling, fold over one third of the omelette in the pan, and then turn it all onto a plate. Another minute for the next one, and you're away. I once cooked forty-four omelettes for a party, one after the other, in an hour, with a collection of different fillings. It's a great trick to learn.

A heavy pan is best. Mine is a Norwegian one, about eight dollars. Don't use it for anything else, and never wash it. If anything sticks, scour it with salt. The more you use it, the better it gets. Lots of butter.

continued

Break 3 eggs in a bowl, add 1 Tbsp water and a
pinch of salt. Beat eggs until stringy and add a
dash of pepper and Tabasco. Heat fry pan until
water bounces on it, melt 2 oz butter in the pan
and add eggs. Stir eggs in a circular motion, moving pan back and forth quickly over high heat. Add
cheese and mushrooms. Turn omelette over a
third, then again, onto the plate.

Some Special Spaghetti from Sicily

Sicily was to be a working breakthrough. I intended to spend two months writing this book—working afternoons. I had visions of a quiet shady bar, a bottle of wine at my elbow and a goat nuzzling my feet. Right after lunch I was going to start; two pages a day and the rest of the time lolling in the lap of the Mediterranean.

But there was a problem. Everybody in Sicily eats lunch. Around 12:30 they start, slowly with a bottle of wine. The local garage mechanic, the coffin maker, the baker, the local lawyer and his mistress, some fishermen—they all take off to a restaurant and they talk. They talk some and eat some, then talk some more and eat some more. Lunch seems to finish around 3:30, unless it's an important one, in which case it might go on until four.

Then it's time for a little rest somewhere behind closed shutters. The bars are not open, the stores are not open, and even the police are nowhere to be seen. There is nothing to do until around five, when the stores and bars open again for a couple of hours, just to fill in the time before dinner. Which is the big meal of the day.

I didn't get any writing done. But I learned an awful lot about spaghetti, and never ate the same dish twice.

Cook spaghetti according to package instructions. Meanwhile chop fine a handful of walnuts and mix with about the same quantity of blue cheese and 1 tsp pepper. Mix well. Chop a handful of parsley. Drain spaghetti and toss with 1 Tbsp butter, walnut mixture and parsley. Serve.

OR, Slice and cube (about the size of sugar cubes) 1 unpeeled eggplant. Fry eggplant in 4 Tbsp good oil, stirring frequently. Chop 3 large or 6 medium tomatoes and add to pan. Add 1 tsp salt, 2 tsp basil, and ½ tsp cayenne pepper. Stir well and cook over medium heat 5 minutes. Add 4 Tbsp good oil, cover and simmer 20 minutes. Stir in 1 glass red wine and cook another 5 minutes. Toss with cooked spaghetti and lots of cheese.

Salade de Haricots Verts au Gruyere

Contrary to popular opinion, what French girls really do is make salads. A simple roast chicken, a salad, some fresh bread and a bottle of wine make a memorable meal, without most of the panic that accompanies North American dinners.

This salad, which, in spring and summer, when the beans are fresh and young, is very close to being one of the greatest salads in the world, is simple, classic, and typically French. It comes (for snob interest) from La Comtesse Guy de Toulouse-Lautrec. On its own it is a very pleasant lunch. With a few trimmings it transforms the simplest dinner.

You can, if you must, use frozen beans. But try it with the fresh ones, the skinniest you can find, the greenest you can find, and the flavour is sophisticated enough for adults, simple enough for children. Make enough. Make lots. It is not a salad to be sneaked on to the corner of a plate and nibbled at.

The secret is in making the vinaigrette—which is simply a French dressing with stuff in it. Once you have made it, it will keep for a long time anywhere reasonably cool. But if you refrigerate it too much,

the oil turns into a lump at the top of the bottle, which requires warming under the hot tap, then shaking.

Put whatever you fancy that is fresh in it. If you use bottled herbs, like tarragon, crush them first between two spoons to liberate the flavour. Shake it a lot. This is another standby which easily becomes a family favourite.

Drop whole prepared green beans in boiled salted water and cook 6 minutes. Drain beans. Combine 1 oz vinegar, ⅔ c olive oil, juice of ½ lemon, 1 tsp salt, ½ tsp pepper, ½ finely chopped onion, 1 tsp chopped parsley, 1 tsp chopped chives, a pinch tarragon and 1 tsp dry mustard (optional) in a bottle and shake. Pour vinaigrette on beans and refrigerate 1 hour. Before serving cut ¼ lb gruyere into ¼-inch cubes and toss with beans.

Cauliflower Cheese

Next time you have vegetarians to dinner, or cauliflowers are cheap, or you have a very simple boiled chicken, try your hand at this.

Just be careful making the sauce. Cook it slowly at first, then add the stock (cubes or real) slowly, and the milk slowly, keeping the temperature up while you do it so that you can see how thick or thin it is getting.

Warm the egg yolks with some of the sauce before you mix them all together (this will stop the yolks curdling), and that's about all you have to worry about. If you want to be really luxurious, use heavy cream instead of the milk, and omit the egg yolks altogether. And if you want to be downright extravagant, use white wine instead of stock.

And if you want to be different, give it a good dusting of nutmeg before you pour the sauce over the cauliflower.

This very simple dish has a habit of becoming a household standby.

Break cauliflower into flowerets and boil in salted water for 7 minutes. Meanwhile melt 2 Tbsp butter, stir in 2 Tbsp flour, and cook 3 minutes over low heat, stirring constantly. Add slowly 1 c hot chicken stock, then 1 c milk. Add 1 tsp salt and pepper to taste. Stir ¼ c hot sauce into 2 beaten egg yolks, then stir back into sauce. Drain cauliflower and sauce. Add 2 Tbsp cheese on top and broil until golden.

Minestra

It seems to vary from north to south; sometimes there's meat in minestra, and sometimes not. This one, a memory of Sicily, is strictly vegetarian, but it's a big, hearty, filling soup nevertheless, and the secret seems to be two kinds of starch. Here we're using beans and potatoes, but it works just as well with beans and rice, or potatoes and pasta.

We used to get through enormous bowls of it with the first bottle of wine because we discovered Sicily in the springtime, where rain makes you wet just like anywhere else, and if you have only summer clothes you get cold like anywhere else. We were sleeping cheap, which meant one toilet for 20 rooms, no bath, only cold water in the sink, and one blanket worn very thin.

Newspapers between the sheet and the blanket rustle a bit, but they warm you at night. Minestra warmed us in the evenings, no matter where we went; big cities or little villages, somebody always had the soup pot on. A good piece of cheese and some fruit make an authentic Italian dessert, and you can spend the money you save on wine.

Pour 3 c boiling water over 1 c dry white beans, and let soak for 30 minutes. Cover and boil beans in soaking water for 30 minutes. Chop 2 medium onions and 6 celery stalks, and cube 2 large, unpeeled potatoes. Add vegetables and 2 bay leaves, ½ tsp pepper, 1 tsp salt, 1 tsp thyme, 4 c water and 1 medium can tomatoes OR 4 or 5 chopped tomatoes to beans. Let simmer 1 hour.

Fagioli Toscanelli con Tonno

The big love of my life sat on a stool in a bookstore. She looked like a missionary who had decided to become a librarian, and she weighed 92 pounds. She drank like a fish, quoted Immanuel Kant, and lived on a steady diet of cinnamon buns. Her refrigerator was full of mould and her kitchen cupboards were stacked from top to bottom with books. There was nothing to eat in her apartment.

I've since discovered that she is not unique. Children leaving home obviously can't carry a set of dishes, a spice rack and a set of copper cooking pots because, apart from anything else, that kind of junk spoils the image. But perhaps a bag of dried beans...

They don't have to be soaked overnight. They don't have to be fussed over. Beans are easy, and once you've accepted that they have an existence completely separate from tomato sauce and miniscule lumps of pork, and that canned beans taste like mush, you are three quarters of the way to being successfully poor.

Let's not go into the nutritionists' spiel, or the stories about Mexicans living on beans and rice. Let's be a little more basic: beans taste good,

they're cheap, and they are good for you. If you don't soak them overnight you can also forget about their musical effect. Don't ask me why, just experiment for yourself. Get a group of friends together. You could even write a thesis. Be my guest. And next time you're in the market, pick up some beans.

Pour 3 c boiling water over 1 c dry white beans and let soak 30 to 45 minutes. Boil the beans for 30 minutes in the soaking water. Chop 1 onion or a bunch of green onions fine. Drain beans and mix with onions. Add a handful of chopped parsley and a small can of tuna. Toss with a mixture of 4 Tbsp oil, 2 Tbsp lemon juice, 1 tsp salt, ½ tsp pepper and ½ tsp of thyme. Serve hot or cold.

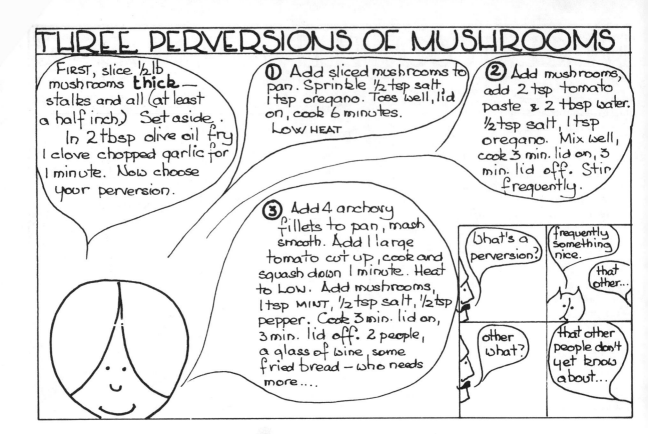

Three Perversions of Mushrooms

The gourmet stores are full of little packets of hideously expensive dried mushrooms imported from the gourmet capitals of the world. Like most dehydrated foods, when the moisture goes most of the flavour goes too, and the mushrooms become pale imitations of the fresh boletus or chanterelles that were originally picked in some Polish or Italian forest. Mushrooms are 90 percent water—not just plain old tap water, but nice flavourful juice. And yet most cooked mushrooms have been fried so thoroughly that the juice has evaporated and they are chewy, tasteless and bland.

Supermarket mushrooms used to be cheap, but not any more. So we should stop treating them as incidentals, or as an accompaniment to steak, and we should give them back a little dignity. Most cookbooks will say, "Don't cook mushrooms in olive oil." Forget that advice and use the best olive oil you can afford—what the Italians call "Extra Virgin"—and be generous with it. (Fry a thick slice of good bread in a couple of tablespoonsful of olive oil, sprinkle on a little salt and pepper, and see for yourself what simple taste is all about.) Be

generous with the herbs and keep the lid on most of the time. Don't overcook mushrooms, and don't be scared to buy the big brown ones because, after all, you don't want them to taste like those canned button mushrooms or you wouldn't be reading this book.

Slice ½ lb mushrooms ½-inch thick and set aside. In 2 Tbsp olive oil fry 1 clove chopped garlic for 1 minute.

Add sliced mushrooms to pan, sprinkle with ½ tsp salt and 1 tsp oregano. Toss well, cover and cook 6 minutes over low heat.

OR, add mushrooms, 2 tsp tomato paste, 2 Tbsp water, ½ tsp salt, and 1 tsp oregano. Mix well and cook 3 minutes covered and 3 minutes uncovered, stirring frequently.

OR, add 4 anchovy fillets to pan, mashed smooth, and 1 large cut up tomato. Reduce heat to simmer. Add mushrooms, 1 tsp mint, ½ tsp salt and ½ tsp pepper. Cook 3 minutes covered and 3 minutes uncovered.

Latkes

Beware of the supermarket pick-up. All those people who used to hang out in discos and prop up the singles bars are now talking gourmet. They lurk in the vegetable section, and talk fancy about zucchini and cold pressed safflower oil; they peer into your shopping basket and come on strong about unsalted butter.

But watch out. All this talk can be learned. Berlitz is now teaching gourmet as an international language to replace Esperanto. There's one sure way to find out if they're bluffing you. Just mention Latkes. There's only one response: "My granma always put a little flour in hers." Anything else is phony, and you should be suspicious.

Of course, if they don't know what latkes are at all, head for the checkout counter immediately. You can't trust nobody these days.

Coarse grate 1 large potato in a bowl. Stir in 1 Tbsp flour, 1 egg, ½ tsp salt and a pinch of pepper. Form pancakes the size of the palm of your hand and fry in 1 Tbsp of oil over medium-high heat. Zucchini and ½ tsp tarragon OR carrots and ½ tsp green dill OR cold rice and ½ tsp curry powder may be substituted in this recipe. Serve as a vegetable or for dessert with sour cream and applesauce.

Chickpeas

Here is the cheapest protein you can buy. Cook your own and they'll have a crunch. If you insist on buying canned ones, drain them, rinse them well to get rid of the slimies, and serve them as if they were real food. Once you discover dried chickpeas (they're no trouble, just put them to soak in water before you go to bed or work) you'll discover all kinds of recipes because people will bring them to you as special gifts. Chickpea people have passwords and a secret handshake. There's a spring in their steps, confidence radiating from their smile. Could it be simply their inner works reacting to the extra protein they're getting? Or is it something more?

Let me tell you that my life has changed since I found chickpeas. And I want you right now to put your hand on this book and let it happen to you. I want you to abandon the earthly pleasures of peanuts and popcorn and come to chickpeas.

Take a bowlful to your next party and see how many converts you make. Like most religions, the central character goes under a variety of names. You might find chickpeas called garbanzos—or even ceci beans.

Soak 1 c dry chickpeas in 4 c water for at least 8 hours. Boil the chickpeas 45 minutes in the soaking water, taking care that they don't boil dry. When the water is almost gone add 1 medium onion chopped fine and 1 clove garlic, chopped. Mix together 4 Tbsp oil, 2 Tbsp lemon juice, 1 tsp salt, ½ tsp pepper and 2 tsp oregano. Stir mixture in with chickpeas.

OR, while the peas cook, fry the onion and garlic over low heat in 2 Tbsp oil with 2 tsp curry powder, 1 tsp salt and 1 Tbsp vinegar. Add this mixture instead of the oil, lemon juice, salt, pepper and oregano.

OR, fry the onion and garlic over low heat, add 1 chopped tomato, a handful chopped parsley, 1 tsp salt, 2 Tbsp oregano, and 2 tsp lemon juice.

Serve hot or cold. Will keep for a week.

Vegetables Vegetables Vegetables

Like the backs of seventeen-year-old knees. Plump and fair and fresh. You have to enjoy vegetables, despite the attempts of the supermarkets to plasticize the experience. All the squeezing (ever watched people putting the half nelson on an avocado?) doesn't really tell you anything; the look should be enough, unless it's a melon you're after, when you have to pick it up and smell it, stick it right under your nose and smell the blunt end, sniff out the perfume—all that genetic inheritance of some distant Persian garden filled with dark-eyed ladies, flying carpets, big black eunuchs with scimitars and an aged gardener sitting quietly in the corner smoking his bhang.

Remember too the Chinese way and don't overcook them. Frozen vegetables are half-digested when you open the packet, so particularly don't overcook them.

I never defrost frozen peas, just dump them straight into the dish, unless I put an ounce of butter in a small saucepan, line it with lettuce leaves, dump in the peas, sprinkle with salt and pepper and a good half teaspoon of dried mint (or some fresh mint leaves), put on the lid and cook at medium heat, shaking frequently, for six or seven minutes.

And rutabagas, those big old yellow old turnips that nobody buys (they keep them in the supermarkets just to confuse the cost of living index) are badly neglected. Eat them raw in thin strips with soy sauce, or mash them with an equal quantity of mashed potatoes, lots of butter and maybe a beaten egg, lots of pepper and some salt.

Carrots—Cut carrots lengthwise into ¼-inch strips. Sprinkle with sugar and cook in 1 Tbsp butter, ½ c water and ½ tsp salt. Cook over medium heat for about 6 minutes. Turn often when water evaporates.

Zucchini—Cut zucchini in ½-inch slices. Fry with garlic over high heat for 2 minutes on each side. Sprinkle with salt and juice of ½ lemon. Cover, lower heat and cook 10 minutes.

continued

Broccoli—Cut broccoli into stalks and boil in ¼ inch salted water, covered, for 3 minutes. Drain and toss with vinaigrette (page 113). Serve hot.

Rutabagas—Peel and cut rutabagas in 1½-inch pieces. Boil in salted water for 15 minutes. Drain well and mash with lots of butter and pepper, salt to taste and an egg yolk.

Go Greek Cheap (comic panels)

Panel 1: go Greek CHEAP

Panel 2: Open a bottle of Retsina and sip it

Panel 3: While you slice Tomatoes. Sprinkle with salt and ground oregano. Place in frig.

Panel 4: drink som more Ret ½ hour later garnish with cubes of FETA

Panel 5: anchovies... thin slivers of green pepper... and green onions in 1" lengths

Panel 6: more Retsina while you make...

Panel 7: TAHINI 3 tbsp. Sesame paste. 1 clove chopped garlic juice of a lemon

Panel 8: These ingredients thicken as they are mixed. Add yogurt until dipping consistency

Panel 9: EAT WITH Greek bread, fingers, more Retsina and the SALAD

Panel 10: preferably by candlelight

Go Greek Cheap

Kids in the Middle East eat more tahini than North American kids eat peanut butter. It's a great sauce for chicken, with soya and a little garlic and maybe some lemon or a little grated ginger, and it's good for fish with white wine, but the nicest and simplest way of eating tahini is simply mixed with yogurt into a stiffish dip.

Tahini is ground sesame seeds. It is sold in most Greek stores and occasional Jewish delicatessens, in cans or in jars, and usually, by the time it gets off the shelf, the oil has separated and come to the top. So mix it with a fork.

Take about four good tablespoonfuls, chop a clove of garlic very fine, and mix it all together with the juice of a lemon. As you add the juice, it will get thick. Don't worry. Now add plain yogurt, a spoonful at a time, mixing it well, until you have a smooth, not too sloppy, dip-consistency bowlful.

Get a loaf of Greek bread, put the tahini in the best looking clay bowl you can find, and pull lumps of the bread. Pick up lots of tahini on the bread and eat it. It will stick to your teeth, which develops the need for retsina. So have a bottle open, and very cold, but don't put it in fancy,

pretty little glasses. Drink it in big mouthfuls. After the first shock, you will love it or hate it. If you don't love it, you'd better go back to peanut butter.

Retsina is just about the worst wine in the world. The first mouthful tastes like paint remover. The second is something else. For some peculiar reason, it is almost hangover-free—which is worth remembering as it is so cheap and goes down so easily. The Greeks used to ship it in barrels of very new, very resinous cypress. At that time it was wine, still very bad wine, but recognizably wine when it started. But by the time it got to wherever it was going, the only taste left was the cypress resin. And people began to recognize it that way, and to like it. So that when it began to be shipped in bottles, they had to add resin to keep the flavour going. It comes in very large bottles, very cheap.

Light the candle (I say candle because I buy altar candles from religious supply stores—a two-foot one looks beautiful and will burn for two or three days). And leave your guests to get on with things while you finish the rest.

continued

Slice some tomatoes (the ripest you can find). Put them on a plate with olive oil, a good sprinkling of salt, and lots of fresh ground oregano. Lots. Then another layer and more of everything. Put it in the fridge for an hour or half an hour. Cut up feta into half-inch cubes, open a can or two of anchovies, cut a green pepper into thin slivers, and cut some green onions into one-inch lengths.

When you are ready, take the tomatoes out of the refrigerator, decorate them with the anchovies, etc., and pour the oil from the anchovies over all. Forks if you must, but fingers are much better. I hope to get Colonel Sanders to try it, then he'll know what finger-lickin' good really means.

One thing more. Get olives, black ones, loose, not canned ones, oily and ripe, and put them with the tomatoes. You will probably need another loaf of bread.

A cheap and honest party.

Slice tomatoes and sprinkle with salt and ground oregano. Let sit in refrigerator for 30 minutes. Add anchovies, thin slivers of green pepper and green onions cut in 1-inch lengths. Meanwhile, combine 3 Tbsp sesame paste, 1 clove chopped garlic and juice of 1 lemon. Add yogurt until sauce reaches dipping consistency. Eat with Greek bread and Retsina.

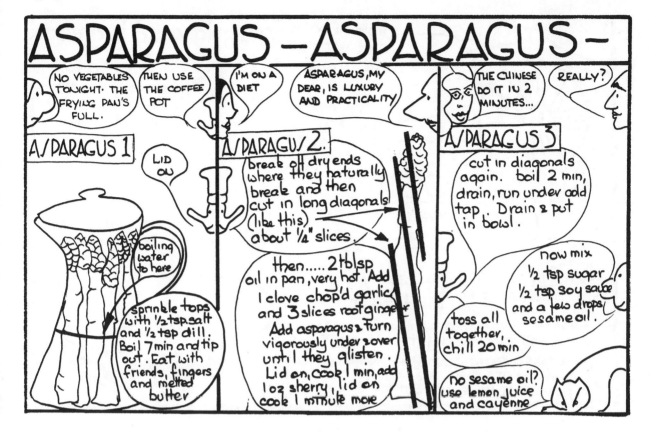

Asparagus-Asparagus

This has nothing at all to do with asparagus in cans or with frozen asparagus, and even less to do with the asparagus of the gourmet kitchens which is peeled and overcooked. This asparagus is the fresh one of early summer and if you live on the West Coast, of late summer too.

This is the asparagus of total luxury, an overindulgence you can afford then and should not attempt to duplicate in midwinter. A couple of slices of ham, if you have to eat meat with it, or a lovely Piccata di Vitello (page 78) if you want to astonish guests with your virtuosity. But basically asparagus is complete unto itself; it makes your life feel better, and gives you some real connection to the great master plan of the universe.

Even the morning after, asparagus reminds you of what a good time you had.

Asparagus 1—Sprinkle asparagus with ½ tsp salt and ½ tsp dill. Boil 7 minutes and drain.

Asparagus 2—Slice asparagus diagonally in ¼-inch slices. Heat 2 Tbsp oil in pan over very hot heat. Add 1 clove chopped garlic, 3 slices ginger root and asparagus. Turn in oil until shiny, cover and cook 1 minute. Add 1 oz sherry, cover and cook 1 minute more.

Asparagus 3—Cut asparagus in diagonals. Boil 2 minutes, drain and refresh under cold water. Drain and put in bowl. Mix ½ tsp sugar, ½ tsp soy sauce and a few drops sesame oil (OR lemon juice seasoned with cayenne). Toss with asparagus and chill 20 minutes.

Mmmushrooms

In the mornings early, before the paperboy, in the fall and in the spring, and on the lawns, the newly made wonderful green billiard table lawns of the newly mortgaged, in subdivisions called Whispering Pines—where perhaps two pines did once, before the bulldozers, exist—there were always mushrooms.

When I was a small boy my uncle showed me where to find mushrooms in cow pastures, and we brought them home, big ones as big as dinner plates and thick as platform shoes. We would cook them slowly, in bacon fat, until they were dark and black, the middles oozing juice, and a smell from them that if bottled and called "Essence de Breakfast" would make a parfumeur's fortune.

If you comb the subdivisons (which have all used topsoil brought in from cow pastures) you are quite likely to find a good crop of field mushrooms at the right time of the year, but you must go early before the crows eat them or before the house-proud owners kick them into the lavender bushes. They taste pretty good, when you can find them. But remember the mushroom picker's creed: When in doubt, chuck it out.

In the supermarkets there are now mushrooms that have not been bleached white—big brownish ones three and four inches across. They are good, too. But the most lily white and virginal mushrooms can also be made into a flavourful, textured, thoroughly dignified meal, instead of just something to add to a steak, if you remember to cook them with the lid on. That was my uncle's secret. Sprinkle them with a little lemon juice if you want to be super-sophisticated, or use basil instead of tarragon. Just be kind and just be gentle.

Remove stems from mushrooms and sprinkle inside cap with salt and tarragon. Meanwhile melt 2 oz butter over medium heat. Lay mushrooms in pan, cover and cook 6 or 7 minutes over low heat. Serve on toast with dribbles of butter. OR, slice small mushrooms thin and toss with 2 Tbsp olive oil, juice of ¼ lemon, ½ tsp salt and 1 tsp oregano. Refrigerate 30 minutes before serving.

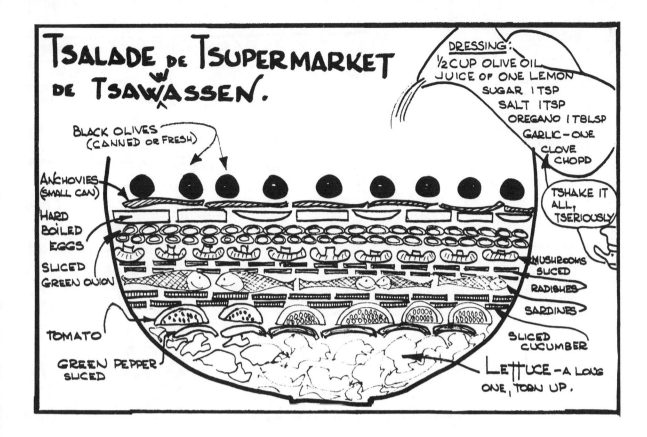

Tsalade de Tsupermarket de Tsawwassen

You have to toss it, and you don't put the dressing on until a minute before you serve it, and before that you have to have the bread ready and the appetites polished and everybody watching, because it looks nice if you've built it carefully, and as you shove your spoons down to the bottom of the bowl and turn up the hidden treasures they are immediately appreciative, just as they are in fancy restaurants when the waiter comes and makes da bigga da fuss with the Caesar Salad.

This is a good summer day supper, very wholesome with a glass of milk if you want to stay holy. You can equally well be sitting on a fire escape or a 47th storey lakeside patio. A salad like this and a decent hamburger (page 26) make a princely meal. (In fact, if any of the princes who visit us have to eat the same rubber chicken as I get served at official functions, then it is a much more than princely meal.)

Tsawwassen? Some of them pronounce it Sawwassen, and tsome of them insist on T-sawwassen. It's in the tsouthwest corner of British Columbia, and is famous for being a five-minute ride from Point Roberts, Washington State's Tijuana.

Layer in a bowl: torn-up lettuce, sliced green pepper, quartered tomato, sliced cucumber, sardines, sliced radishes, sliced mushrooms, sliced green onion, sliced hard boiled eggs, small can anchovies and black olives. For dressing combine ½ c olive oil, juice of 1 lemon, 1 tsp sugar, 1 tsp salt, 1 Tbsp oregano and 1 chopped clove garlic. Shake dressing.

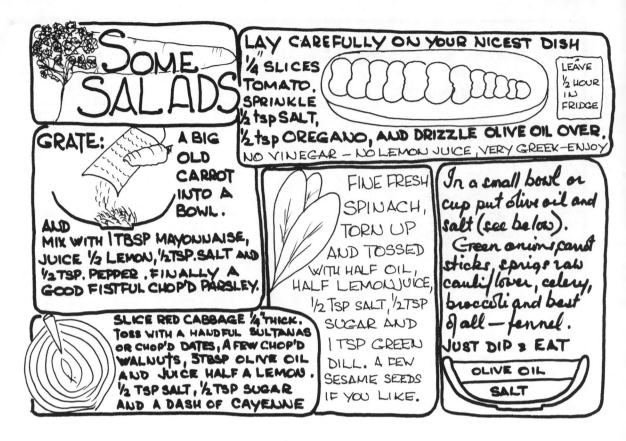

SOME SALADS

LAY CAREFULLY ON YOUR NICEST DISH
¼" SLICES TOMATO. SPRINKLE ½ tsp SALT,
½ tsp OREGANO, AND DRIZZLE OLIVE OIL OVER.
NO VINEGAR — NO LEMON JUICE, VERY GREEK—ENJOY

LEAVE ½ HOUR IN FRIDGE

GRATE: A BIG OLD CARROT INTO A BOWL.
AND MIX WITH 1 TBSP MAYONNAISE, JUICE ½ LEMON, ½ TSP. SALT AND ½ TSP. PEPPER. FINALLY A GOOD FISTFUL CHOP'D PARSLEY.

FINE FRESH SPINACH, TORN UP AND TOSSED WITH HALF OIL, HALF LEMON JUICE, ½ TSP SALT, ½ TSP SUGAR AND 1 TSP GREEN DILL. A FEW SESAME SEEDS IF YOU LIKE.

In a small bowl or cup put olive oil and salt (see below). Green onions, carrot sticks, sprigs raw cauliflower, celery, broccoli and best of all — fennel. JUST DIP & EAT

OLIVE OIL
SALT

SLICE RED CABBAGE ¼" THICK. TOSS WITH A HANDFUL SULTANAS OR CHOP'D DATES, A FEW CHOP'D WALNUTS, 3 TBSP OLIVE OIL AND JUICE HALF A LEMON. ½ TSP SALT, ½ TSP SUGAR AND A DASH OF CAYENNE

Some Salads

Edith Sitwell was a snotty, uppity, frightfully rich and even more pretentious lady of the avant-garde art scene in Britain who (along with Dylan Thomas and sundry other literary drunks) was among the first of the electronic age shock troops to visit North America and lecture to the culture hungry.

When she went back to England her friends said, "Tell us dahling, do tell us about America." "My deahs," she replied, "it was one cocktail party after another."

"And what" (the Brits are rather like this) they asked, "is a cocktail party?"

"Peanuts," she answered. "Peanuts, whiskey and an infinity of boredom."

But they pressed her even more for some facts concerning life on this side of the Atlantic. Any fact, in fact.

"Well, my deahs," (and nobody ever worked out whether it was her eyebrows which pulled her nose up or the nose which pushed from beneath) "it appeared to me that at any given moment fifty percent of the population was eating the same dreary lettuce."

It doesn't have to be, it doesn't have to be, despite what your Home Ec teacher told you.

Tomatoes—Lay ¼-inch tomato slices on a serving plate and sprinkle with ½ tsp salt and ½ tsp oregano. Drizzle with olive oil. Let set ½ hour in the refrigerator before serving.

Carrots—Grate a large carrot into a bowl. Mix 1 Tbsp Mayonnaise, juice of ½ lemon, ½ tsp sale, ½ tsp pepper and a handful of chopped parsley.

Cabbage—Slice cabbage ¼ inch thick. Toss it with a handful bultanas or chopped dates, a few chopped walnuts, 3 Tbsp olive oil and juice of ½ lemon, ½ tsp salt, ½ tsp sugar and a dash of cayenne.

Spinach—Toss torn up fresh spinach with a mixture of 1 part oil to 1 part lemon juice, ½ tsp salt, ½ tsp sugar and 1 tsp dill (sesame seeds optional).

Olive oil—Mix good olive oil and salt to taste. Use as a dip.

Salad Dressings

It's not all that complicated, you don't need a $200 Cuisinart, or a twenty-speed blender, not even a fancy French whip. All you need to free yourself forever from the bondage of the bottled salad dressings (you know how they hang around in the fridge, an inch of blue cheese and a bit less of Italian and some weird stuff that the label fell off of and you don't know whether it's suntan lotion gone sour or the cream that Doctor Whatsit gave you the time you both went to see him but it was a false alarm), all you need is a spice jar, one of those nice little ones that the Spice Islands oregano comes in.

Put the stuff in, screw the lid on—unless you want your friends to lick the dressing off *you*—and shake it well. That's all. (You can use the same technique for blending flour or cornstarch and water to thicken a sauce.)

Just shake it well, stick your finger in to taste it, and fix it up the way your tongue tells you to, remembering never to put it on green salads until just before you're going to eat. That way the greens stay fresh.

Use 2 measures of good oil for every 1 measure of lemon juice, OR wine OR vinegar. Add ½ tsp salt, a pinch of pepper and a little garlic. Add 1 tsp of oregano, OR mint, OR dill, OR tarragon, OR thyme. Taste and add a bit of sugar, if desired. Beat in 1 egg yolk. See serving suggestions above.

Ginger Tea

This needs friends, and a candle too is nice, and a good dinner first is great, and wine is always wine.

For each person: A mugful of water, an inch or so of fresh root ginger grated course into the saucepan, two heaped teaspoons brown sugar or a bit more honey), and half a lemon (peel and all). Boil (lid on) ten to fifteen minutes.

Pour (strained—just hold back the shreds with something) into mugs and drink as hot as you can. The first sip liberates your taste buds (the Japanese do the same thing with sliced ginger for sushi), the second (which should be a good mouthful) clears your head, and half way through the cup you should get off—nice and warm and loose.

For each person: Combine in a saucepan 1 mugful water, an inch or so fresh grated ginger, 2 tsp brown sugar and ½ lemon with peel. Boil, covered 10 to 15 minutes. Pour through strainer and drink hot.

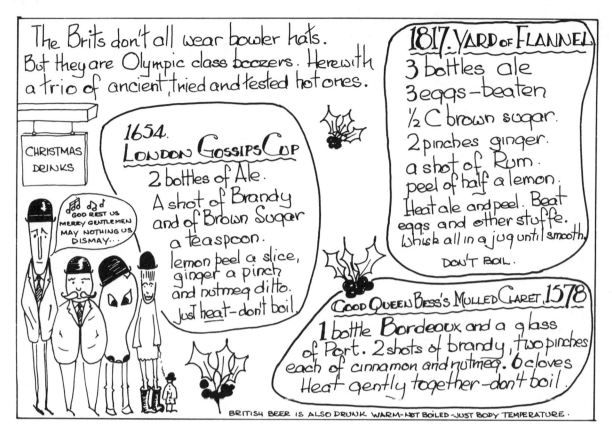

The Brits don't all wear bowler hats. But they are Olympic class boozers. Herewith a trio of ancient, tried and tested hot ones.

CHRISTMAS DRINKS

♪♪♪ GOD REST US MERRY GENTLEMEN MAY NOTHING US DISMAY...

1654.
LONDON GOSSIPS CUP
2 bottles of Ale.
A shot of Brandy and of Brown Sugar a teaspoon.
lemon peel a slice, ginger a pinch and nutmeg ditto.
Just heat - don't boil.

1817. YARD OF FLANNEL
3 bottles ale
3 eggs - beaten
½ C brown sugar.
2 pinches ginger.
a shot of Rum.
peel of half a lemon.
Heat ale and peel. Beat eggs and other stuffe.
Whisk all in a jug until smooth.
DON'T BOIL.

GOOD QUEEN BESS'S MULLED CLARET. 1578
1 bottle Bordeaux and a glass of Port. 2 shots of brandy, two pinches each of cinnamon and nutmeg. 6 cloves Heat gently together - don't boil.

BRITISH BEER IS ALSO DRUNK WARM - NOT BOILED - JUST BODY TEMPERATURE.

Christmas Drinks

Hot tea is the simplest of all hot drinks. My grandmother loved it. With half an inch of whiskey in the bottom of the cup. I still do it, on Sunday afternoons, when it's raining. And the same amount of brandy in a cup of coffee has considerable merit.

But it seems that Christmas time is the time for getting sentimental about hot toddies, and punches, and Wassail Bowls, so most people get out a tin saucepan and a bottle of the cheapest, and boil it with cinnamon or detergent or whatever takes their fancy, and drink it quick and spend the next days bragging about their hangovers.

Next time you make a hot drink, try using your best booze, and your best saucepan, and don't boil it, just make it hot enough in small quantities, and find your way into a pleasant warm nodding happiness.

And if you want a very pleasant occupation, try Charles Baker's English Bishop. First you take an orange and stud it all over with whole cloves. Dip it in brandy and roll it in brown sugar. Put it on a stick and toast it over the fire until the sugar caramelizes. Now cut it into quarters, put it in a pan with a bottle of the best port you can find, and just simmer very gently for twenty minutes with the lid on. Add four ounces of brandy, and warm another ounce in a spoon. Just before you serve it, pour the brandy (the spoon-warm brandy) gently on to the saucepan and set fire to it. Very potent. But you must not boil it; boiling ruins any wine for drinking, and port most of all. Happy Christmas.

Gossip's Cup—Combine 2 bottles ale, 1 Tbsp brandy, 1 tsp brown sugar, 1 slice lemon peel, 1 pinch ginger and 1 pinch nutmeg, and heat, but do not boil.

Yard of Flannel—Combine 3 bottles ale and peel of ½ lemon and heat. Beat together 3 eggs, ½ c brown sugar, ⅓ tsp ginger and ½ c rum. Mix egg mixture with ale until smooth. Do not boil.

Good Queen Bess Mulled Claret—Combine, cover and heat, but do not boil: 3 c claret, 1 c port, ½ c cognac, peel of 1 lemon, 2 pinches each cinammon and nutmeg, and 6 cloves.

Hot Doughnuts for Breakfast

The early morning zombie's solution to breakfast. Leave the Eggs Benedict to the professionals, don't spoil your lunch with kippers or kedgeree, and don't pretend that porridge is anything more than mush. Take it easy in the mornings—sprinkle a little ground coffee on the burner of your stove, just to perfume the kitchen, and make something simple.

These little doughnuts are the ultimate simplicity, and they are virtually foolproof. In their original version, they were known (quite respectably) as *Pets de Nonne,* which literally translated means Nun's farts. Should you, out of delicacy, prefer the original pre-eighteenth century French, it was *Pets de Pute,* which means Whore's farts.

They are light, airy, delicate, and they don't keep.

Bring ½ c water, 1 tsp sugar, 4 Tbsp butter and ¼ tsp salt to boil in a pan and immediately take off heat. Add ½ c flour all at once and stir well. Add two eggs, one at a time, mixing vigorously with a fork until smooth. Cook, over lowest heat, stirring until it doesn't stick to sides of the pan. Heat 1 c oil in a small fry pan or a saucepan. Slide teaspoonfuls of batter into the oil and fry until medium brown, turning twice. Do not crowd. Remove cooked doughnuts with a fork and sprinkle with sugar. Serve hot.

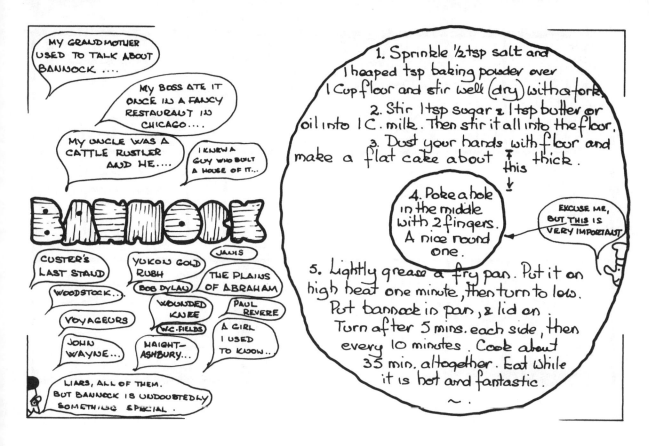

Bannock

Hollywood used to insist that the West was won with the Colt .45 and the rather convenient habit the Bad Guys had of always wearing black Stetsons, which enabled the Good Guys, who were none too bright, to recognize them and hit them over the head with a chair.

But I became convinced at an early age that the real key to survival in cowboy country was bannock, the legendary bread that camp cooks made in th' embers of a dyin' fire, and the cowpokes wolfed down with their dawn coffee. Every grade B Western I saw had bannock in it somewhere; so did the Western magazines, and so did all the outdoor cookbooks. For years I tried to make it. I followed all the instructions, I bought hand-milled flour, and once I even carried water from the "crick" in m' cowboy hat. But nothin' worked. All I got were sodden lumps with a burned outside, too heavy for a Frisbee and too hard for a cushion.

I figgered that the Code of the West, which came out strong against all sorts of dishonourable behaviour, didn't extend to lyin' about campfire bread. So instead of ridin' off into the sunset, I went Bad and took to kissin' Miss Emmy, even stayin' overnight.

The League of Cowboys for the Code couldn't, by their constitution, gun me down, and I never go into bars that have chairs, so they finally came up with this here recipe, and asked me to mend my ways.

It works. The hole is the secret because it lets the heat into the previously soggy middle. It's crusty, it's wonderful with butter, and the only problem is that Miss Emmy likes it so much she reckons I ought to stay every night.

Sprinkle ½ tsp salt and 1 heaping tsp baking powder over 1 c flour and stir well with a fork. Combine 1 tsp sugar and 1 tsp butter or oil into 1 c milk. Stir milk mixture into flour mixture. Dust your hands with flour and make a flat cake about ½-inch thick. Poke a hole in the middle with 2 fingers. Lightly grease a fry pan, heat it over high heat 1 minute, then reduce heat to low. Put bannock in pan and cover. Turn after 5 minutes on each side, then every 10 minutes. Cook about 35 minutes total. Eat hot.

Le Big Secret

Just think of them as pancakes and it's easy. Not hotcakes, but just some rather special pancakes that you are going to make for a weekend breakfast or lunch. Then, if you want to show off one day with a great flaming flourish at the end of dinner, you will know how. Your guests will be impressed, and you may well have learned a new social grace—such as what to say to the boss the morning after you have set his wife's wig on fire.

Crepes or pancakes, the mix is the same:

7 ounces flour
3 eggs
1 teaspoon sugar
¾ pint milk
A good pinch of salt
2 tablespoons melted butter
1 ounce cognac or rum

The rum is essential for crepes, optional for pancakes. In either case, nice.

Mix the flour, sugar, and salt in one bowl. Beat together the eggs, milk, butter and cognac in another bowl—and slowly mix them into the dry ingredients. Keep beating until everything is smooth. Don't bother with a beater. Use a fork.

Now leave it at least two hours, or overnight in the refrigerator. Just ignore it. That's all the making there is. The rest is cooking.

For pancakes, check that the mixture is thin. If it is any thicker than cream, add water and mix in with a fork until it's thin enough.

Heat your cast iron pan on a medium heat. Melt about half a teaspoon of butter all over the pan, and pour in enough batter to cover the bottom thinly. Swirl it about a bit so it does cover. The mix should be thin enough to run.

Cook about a minute, and turn it over with a spatula or (all this needs is courage and nobody looking) toss it. Another minute and it will be done.

Sprinkle sugar all over, squeeze about a quarter of a lemon on the sugar, roll it up in a pan and roll it on to a plate. A little more sugar, a little more lemon juice, and you have the traditional English pancake.

Crepes you cook the same way in a little pan. And you stack them up until you have about three

continued

per person. It's best to do it in the afternoon if you insist on showing off at dinner.

You can fill them with smoked salmon, or crab, and cook them in a Hollandaise sauce, or you can be really vulgar and ostentatious and do the whole crepes suzette trip. Whatever you do will be expensive.

For crepes suzette, cream a quarter-pound butter with three good tablespoonfuls sugar (icing sugar is best), a tablespoon of grated lemon rind, and the rind and the juice of an orange. And about an ounce of Cointreau (or Grand Marnier or Curacao).

Really cream the butter and sugar. Then add the other things slowly, and keep mixing. If it separates, don't worry too much. The heat will fix things for you.

Heat the big heavy pan, dump in the butter mixture, and cook it until it bubbles. Then dip each little crepe from the pre-cooked stack into the mixture, turn it over, fold it into quarters, and push it to one side of the pan.

When they are all done, spread them back over the pan, sprinkle them with sugar, and pour about an ounce of brandy and Cointreau (or whatever) on them. Stand back, light a match, and whoosh. Easy and expensive.

Mix together 7 oz flour, 1 tsp sugar and pinch of salt in one bowl. Beat together 3 eggs, ¾ pt milk, 2 Tbsp butter and 1 oz cognac or rum. Slowly mix liquid and flour mixture until smooth. Let stand 2 hours or overnight in the refrigerator. Heat cast iron pan over medium heat. Melt ½ tsp butter in pan and pour in enough batter to thinly cover the bottom. Cook about 1 minute, turn and cook for another minute. See serving suggestions above.

P-seudo P-sourdough P-sancakes

These pancakes are a Saturday or Sunday indulgence, when you have time enough for one of you to stay in bed, while the other sits and reads the paper. There is nothing to the cooking of the pancakes; you just cook one side till there are bubbles on the top, turn it over and cook the other side and eat them with hot maple syrup and butter. They will keep warm wrapped in a cloth in a low oven until you get enough, or if you happen to have your bed in the kitchen you can just eat them as they come. There are people who spend Saturday night on an air mattress on the kitchen floor just to be there in the morning, but that is close to addiction, which, until a local chapter of Pancakes Anonymous is formed, should be avoided.

But there are other aspects of these pancakes which should be noted. The first one up makes tea, peels an orange, gets the morning paper down off the roof, and delivers these three things, preferably with a flower and a candle, to the bedside. He then puts on the coffee while he makes the pancake mixture, feeds the cat, avoids last night's dishes, and (this is a secret) sprinkles dry coffee on the stove burner so that the whole apartment begins to smell like coffee should taste.

By the time the coffee is ready the pancakes will be ready to cook. You know how to do this. Now, the first one you will have to try. Just to see if it is good enough for your mate. It will be. And perhaps that, you will think, was an accident, and you should try the next one. So you mix another batch, and finally deliver them, smiling, together with the maple syrup (if you can find Swedish lingonberries in a delicatessen then so much the better than anything else in the world), and butter, and hot coffee, and of course yourself, a portable radio and a couple of spare cushions.

The greatest pleasure comes in not answering the phone or the doorbell.

Beat 3 eggs and add 1 c flour, 6 oz yoghurt and 1 c milk. Still beating, add 2 Tbsp sugar, 1 tsp salt, 2 tsp baking powder and 4 Tbsp oil or melted butter. Let stand 10 minutes before cooking.

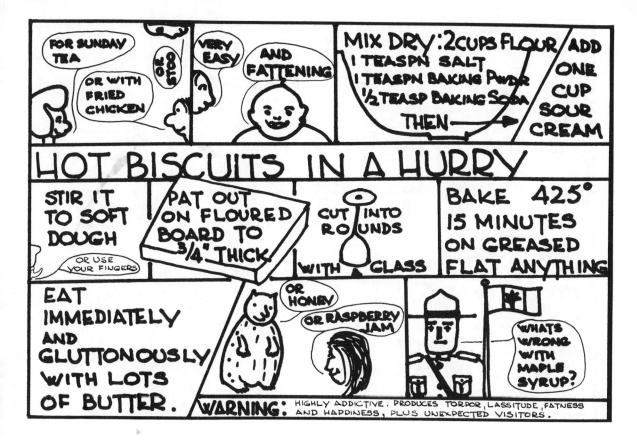

Hot Biscuits in a Hurry

Nothing looks more competent in a kitchen than baking. And there is nothing more rewarding for so little effort. A bit of flour, a bit of baking powder, a bowl, some fat and some milk, five minutes messing, fifteen minutes in the oven and there it is, hot and indigestible and a statement of love.

If you are going to graduate to bread, start with biscuits. You can be impressive at breakfast with them (or even more impressive in bed), very grandmotherly at teatime by the fire, and extremely economical at supper time with a poor man's soup and a basketful of hot biscuits.

When you take them out of the oven put a cloth in the bottom of a bowl, then the biscuits, then wrap the ends of the cloth over to keep them warm.

And if it's two o'clock in the morning and you're hungry, try this instead of sending out for a pizza.

Mix 2 c flour, 1 tsp salt, 1 tsp baking powder, ½ tsp baking soda and 1 c sour cream. Pat dough out on floured board to ¾-inch thick. Cut in rounds and bake for 15 minutes in a 425 degree oven on a greased cookie sheet.

Just Enough Jam

My grandmother lived in the same house for fifty-seven years. It was the jam that kept her there. She was good at it, and also miserly. The cupboards of her kitchen, the tops of her closets, the basement, even suitcases under the bed, were full of jam. Strawberry jam, blackberry jam, marrow and ginger jam, rhubarb jam and even turnip jam. If we were very good we were allowed to eat it, on fresh bread, which she was also very good at.

Nobody wants an apartment full of jam today, but it is nice, each time a new summer fruit appears fresh in the stores, to make it just once, just enough for a couple of breakfasts or tea with some friends. Or pancakes.

This way of making jam is foolproof, and it tastes nice, without any of the pectin or other mystiques that usually seem to go into jam making.

If you buy strawberries by the pound, then the proportions are correct. If you buy a twelve ounce packet, which for some reason appears to be popular with the supermarkets, then use 2¼ cups of sugar and most of the juice of the lemon.

You can put the rest in gin.

And if you want to be super conservative, peel the lemon first in a long thin continuous spiral, just the yellow part, before you squeeze it. Then poke it into a mickey of gin, and leave it for a week or two. Nice, clean-tasting lemon gin—very good for summer.

Most other summer fruits will also make jam. Just use three-quarters of the sugar you do for strawberries.

Combine 1 lb hulled and not-too-ripe strawberries, 3 c berry sugar and juice of 1 lemon in a very heavy saucepan. Bring to a slow boil and then boil fast for 6 minutes, stirring constantly. Put in jars.

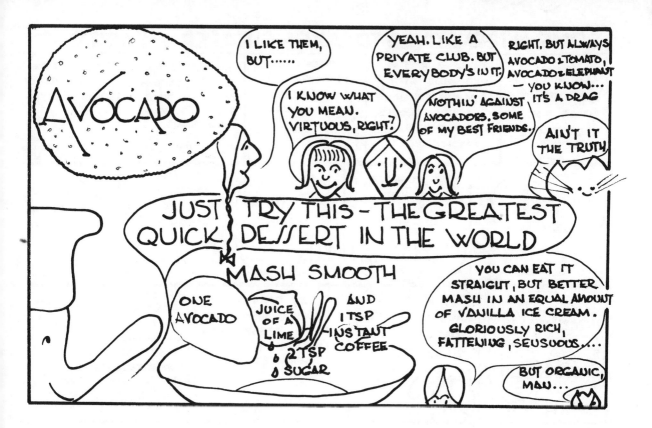

Avocado

This dessert is God's way of saying She's sorry for inventing instant coffee.

Mash 1 avocado smooth with the juice of 1 lime, 2 Tbsp sugar and 1 tsp instant coffee. Mash in an equal amount of vanilla ice cream and serve cold.

Some Cheaper and Easier Alternatives to Cake

Desserts tyrannize most social meals. People work their butts off to make something unusual and wonderful for supper; they shop and cook and worry and spoil their sex lives for days ahead, and before their guests are halfway through the soup they're speculating on what the dessert will be, talking about a wonderful cake that Valerie made, and refusing second helpings "so I'll have room for dessert."

It seems almost obligatory to make something rich and creamy, indigestible and fattening. I prefer the desserts of Italy, where fruit is slowly and elegantly peeled and savoured, but occasionally I muck about with my fruit, make pretties of it, and serve very small portions. These three suggestions will in no way reduce your reputation, and you won't have to sit there fuming while some oaf (usually the one who smokes between courses) raves over a cake that two hours before was in the frozen foods section of the local market.

Besides, any leftovers are fine for breakfast, and no matter how depraved you might be, you can't eat cake at 7:00 a.m.

Pears—Peel and quarter 1 pear for each 2 people. Boil ¼ bottle red wine with 3 slices fresh ginger, 4 cloves and a squeeze lemon juice. (May substitute powdered ginger for fresh and cinnamon for cloves.) Simmer pears 20 minutes, remove from pan and boil wine down fast, 2 to 3 minutes. Pour sauce over pears and eat hot or cold.

Apples—Peel and quarter apples and slice thin. Lay apple slices in 3 Tbsp plain yogurt in a bowl. Squeeze with lemon juice, dribble with maple syrup and sprinkle with sesame seeds.

Oranges—Cut unpeeled juice oranges crosswise into ¼-inch slices. Layer them in a bowl and sprinkle with 2 Tbsp sugar for each person. Pour 1 oz of rum for each person over oranges and let marinate for 1 hour or more.

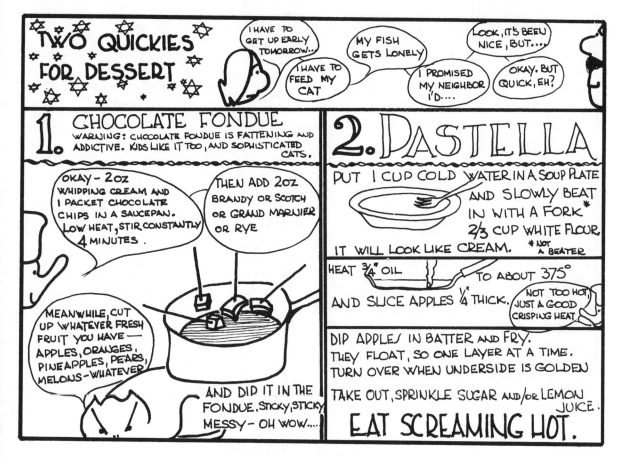

Two Quickies for Dessert

You don't have to invite people in for *dinner*. Let them get it elsewhere. Ask them to come around nine (which is when the real talk starts anyway) for dessert.

They arrive full of their own booze, with food they chose themselves; they're happy (and so are you because you spent two hours in the bath, both of you listening first to a little Brahms, perhaps the Clarinet Quintet, and then the Dvorak Cello Concerto, the Fournier one) and they are anticipatory, because everybody waits for dessert.

Which is the ideal climate for entertaining. You should of course be careful, if you live alone, not to fall into the habit of making chocolate fondue just for yourself, because that way lies chocoholism, the dread disease of once slender blondes who have to run miles every day to keep the symptoms from showing.

Even after a movie—four of you—it's easy enough to pick up some chocolate chips in the all-night store. Everybody loves dessert. As the Anglos say in Quebec, *chacun à son "goo."*

Chocolate Fondue—Combine 2 oz whipping cream and 1 packet chocolate chips in a saucepan. Stir constantly over low heat for 4 minutes. Add 2 oz brandy, OR scotch, OR Grand Marnier, OR rye. Cut up a variety of fresh fruit and dip in fondue.

Pastella—Slowly beat in ⅔ c white flour into 1 c of cold water in a soup plate. Heat ¾ inches oil to about 375 degrees. Slice apples ¼-inch thick. Dip apples in batter and fry, one layer at a time. Turn when underside is golden. Take out, sprinkle with sugar and lemon juice (optional).

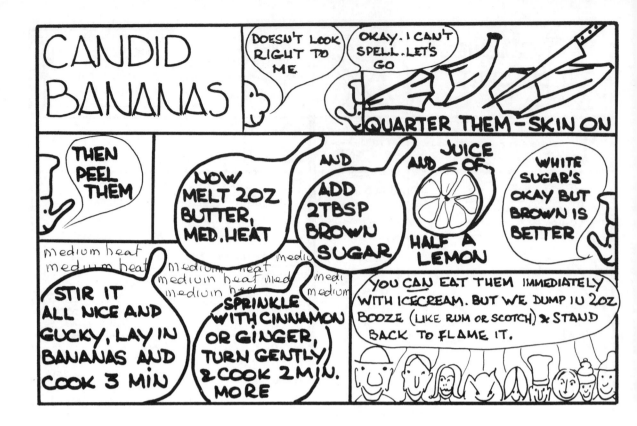

Candid Bananas

Candid. Up front. Open. Honest. This is a dessert ridiculously simple, disgustingly rich, gloriously calorific and, because of the ready availability of bananas, habit-forming. Just be a little careful, don't have the heat too high, take them out of the pan with the same care you would offer a day-old baby (anybody who has ever carried a baby about on a spoon will know exactly what I mean) and serve them on warm plates. Don't cook too many at a time; three bananas is enough for the average pan, and besides, it does your guests good to wait for seconds. And thirds.

Quarter bananas, skin on; then peel them. Melt 2 oz butter over medium heat and add 2 Tbsp brown sugar and the juice of ½ lemon. Stir and cook 3 minutes. Sprinkle with cinnamon OR ginger, turn gently and cook 2 minutes more. See serving suggestions above.

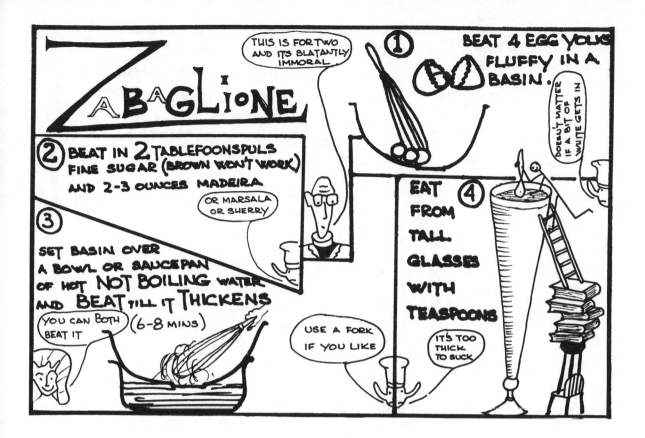

Zabaglione

Zabaglione is the only dessert anybody needs to know. It is the best food in the world for two, sensual, easy, rich, mildly intoxicating and so nice that no matter what you have done with the rest of the dinner it will be forgiven and forgotten.

The making is foolproof, if you take care of just two things. It is nice to get the egg whites and yolks separated, but it doesn't matter if you are a bit sloppy. It is nice to use fresh eggs that haven't been in the refrigerator, but it doesn't matter that much. It is nice to use Marsala, but sherry is okay and so is Madeira. I know people who have developed a taste for it with whiskey, but none of these things really matters. What is important is to keep beating it, and not to use boiling water.

I just take a saucepan of boiling water off the stove and use that, topping it up occasionally to keep it hot. If you leave the bottom of the bowl unbeaten while you light cigarettes or display your etchings it will curdle or turn into a custard. Which has no appeal at all.

It has been around a long time as a food and an aphrodisiac. The Romans like it, and the Italians, and the French and the Spaniards. I have had a Greek version of it made with that aromatic Greek honey (this needs a lot of care and a lot of beating), and in Belgium a Dutch bottled version of it is very popular. But best of all it is fresh made, and eaten very quietly, at body temperature.

Beat 4 eggs fluffy in a bowl. Beat in 2 Tbsp fine white sugar and 2 to 3 oz Madeira, OR Marsala OR sherry. Put bowl over a bowl or saucepan of hot, but not boiling, water. Beat until it thickens, 6 to 8 minutes. Serve just warm.

Ice Cream and Whiskey

Oh those pillow-warm and plumply pretty
  girls who live in every city
    never whistled at by any
      men who think it highly bene-
        ficial to their status
          to take out girls not quite so fat as
           the placid, kind and all-forgiving
             chubbies who think cheesecake's living.

Top each serving of vanilla ice cream with ½ tsp instant coffee and ½ tsp cocoa powder. Finish with 1 Tbsp whiskey.

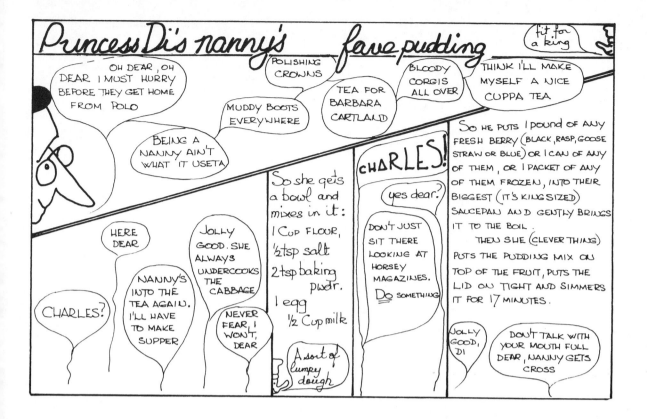

Princess Di's Nanny's Fave Pudding

You can be a convicted dope dealer, a politician, a mugger of the elderly or a stealer of babies' rattles, a stockbroker, wiretapper, hangman, bank manager, even a baseball umpire—but if you can make a decent pudding, you're acceptable in any society. There's something so virtuous about pudding, something utterly wholesome. It's the good old days all over again with your stomach purring "thank you."

If you're ashamed of the simple virtues and insist on the sophistications of the gourmet set, put an ounce or two of booze in with the fruit, or a squirt or two of lemon. You can slice apples to go with the berries, or use jam thinned with water; you can pour cream over it all, or custard. And you can even not make a dessert at all but put leftover curry in the bottom of the pan with a little water, or leftover stew, dump the dough on top, and there it is: a meat pudding just waiting for a little salad to be a complete dinner.

You don't have to go to private school, or have nanny, or be rich...

Mix 1 c flour, ½ tsp salt, 2 tsp baking powder, 1 egg and ½ c milk. Put 1 lb fresh berries, OR 1 can berries, OR 1 packet frozen berries into a large pan, bring to a boil, and add milk mixture. Cover and simmer for 17 minutes.